# The Manager's Guide to
# Enterprise Security Risk Management:
## Essentials of Risk-Based Security

## Brian Allen, Esq.

### CISSP, CISM, CPP, CFE

## Rachelle Loyear

### CISM, MBCP

### Kristen Noakes-Fry, ABCI, Editor

ISBN 978-1-944480-25-7 PDF

ISBN 978-1-944480-24-0 EPUB

ISBN 978-1-944480-52-3 PRINT

ROTHSTEIN PUBLISHING
A Division of Rothstein Associates Inc.

Brookfield, Connecticut USA

203.740.7400 • 203.740.7401 fax

info@rothstein.com

www.rothstein.com

**ISBN 978-1-944480-25-7 PDF**

**ISBN 978-1-944480-24-0 EPUB**

**ISBN 978-1-944480-52-3 PRINT**

**Library of Congress Control Number 2018942973**

ROTHSTEIN PUBLISHING
A Division of Rothstein Associates Inc.

**Brookfield, Connecticut USA**

**203.740.7400 • 203.740.7401 fax**

**info@rothstein.com**

www.rothstein.com

***Keep informed about Rothstein Publishing:***
**www.facebook.com/RothsteinPublishing**
**www.linkedin.com/company/rothsteinpublishing**
**www.twitter.com/rothsteinpub**

# CONTENTS

# Part 1

# What Is Enterprise Security Risk Management (ESRM) And How Can It Help You?

**This part will help you to:**

> ➤ Understand what is meant by Enterprise Security Risk Management.
> ➤ Explain the difference between traditional, task-based management and strategic, risk-based management.
> ➤ Understand and overcome some of the blocks to effective relationships with enterprise leaders.
> ➤ See how adopting ESRM can lead to a more successful security program overall and enhance your own career.

# What is Enterprise Security Risk Management (ESRM)?

As a security practitioner, you know the world is a risky place, and you know it's becoming more risk filled all the time. Hardly a day goes by without headlines about a workplace shooting, a data breach, a cyber-attack, or some other security failure that has exposed an enterprise and its assets – human, physical, and intangible – to some kind of serious risk. Whatever your security role, and no matter how far along you are in your security career, it's your responsibility to protect your enterprise, and its assets, against these high-profile threats, and many others that are only beginning to emerge and be recognized. These changes in the security risk environment, and the urgent changes they require in your work as a security practitioner, are the reason we wrote this book.

This book is about an approach to security that's new and yet familiar, radical and yet practical: enterprise security risk management (ESRM).

## 1.1 ESRM Defined

We'll be discussing the meaning and implications of ESRM in depth throughout this book, but let's begin at the beginning, with a simple, straightforward definition of the term:

> **Enterprise security risk management is the application of fundamental risk principles to manage all security risks – whether information, cyber, physical security, asset management, or business continuity – in a comprehensive, holistic, all-encompassing approach.**

To break that down further, we can look at the individual parts of the definition.

### 1.1.1 Enterprise

An *enterprise* is a business or company.

This can be a:

- Public, state or government run organization.
- A privately held, family company.
- A not-for-profit organization providing goods, services, or other non-profit activities.
- A stockholder controlled corporation.

- Any other organization that exists to fulfill a purpose defined by that organization.

When we reference business, organization, company, or any similar term in this book, we are referring to any or all of the above – an enterprise.

### 1.1.2 Security Risk

*Security risk* is anything that threatens harm to the enterprise, its mission, its employees, customers, or partners, its operations, its reputation.

That can mean:

- A troubled employee with a gun.
- An approaching hurricane.
- A computer hacker in another country.
- A dissatisfied customer with a social media account and too much time on his or her hands.
- And, of course, many more.

Security risks take many different forms, and new ones are being introduced all the time. Recognizing those risks, making them known to the enterprise, and helping your internal functional business partners mitigate them is central to the ESRM philosophy.

### 1.1.3 Risk Principles

The definition of ESRM states that risks are *managed* through fundamental risk principles. Here, we'll reference an already existing body of knowledge on how to manage all types of risk, and apply it specifically to the security function. There are well-established, fundamental risk principles – principles that have been tested and found effective over many years, in many different enterprises, and in many different industries – that can be used to manage risks of all types.

The International Organization for Standardization, in standard *ISO 31000:2009 – Risk management – Principles and guidelines*, and the American National Standards Institute, in their standard document *ANSI/ASIS/RIMS RA.1-2015 – Risk Assessment*, both outline similar, highly effective, standards for risk management. A few examples of key principles from the ISO standard 31000 (2009) are that risk management should:

- Be part of the decision-making process.
- Be transparent and inclusive.
- Be dynamic, iterative, and responsive to change.
- Be capable of continual improvement and enhancement.

Again, these are just a few snippets from the standard. The entire standard is voluminous and comprehensive and we'll describe more from this risk standard and others in the course of this book to give you a road map showing how to use these fundamental principles of risk management and apply them to the security risks you are responsible for managing.

## 1.2 How is ESRM Different from Traditional Security?

The description of ESRM above may sound somewhat like what you and your security organization are already doing – and the fact is, you probably are already doing some parts of it. So let's take a look at what makes ESRM such a radical departure from traditional, "conventional" security. To do that, we need a baseline understanding of what traditional security is – and what it is not.

These days, security practitioners are often too busy dealing with threats and vulnerabilities and other urgent operational problems to ask themselves basic questions about what they do and why they do it.

Questions like:

- What is my role in the business environment, beyond the specific security tasks I've been assigned?
- Why are the tasks I do every day necessary for the enterprise?
- How is what I do perceived in the organization?
- What is the mission my department is chartered to accomplish?

That's a serious problem, because in security, as in every other business discipline, if you aren't sure what you're trying to accomplish – why you're doing what you're doing – you can't be sure you're doing it right. And, just as important, you can't be sure that you're being recognized by the management in your organization as doing it right.

### 1.2.1 Traditional Corporate Security Scenarios: Something is Missing

One thing we've learned in our years as security professionals is that there are a lot of different ways to "do security." Some are good, some are bad, most are a bit of both – and all can teach us something about how to do things better. We've talked to a lot of security managers and practitioners in our time, at conferences, seminars, and other industry events, and we've learned about a lot of different approaches to security. Here are just a few things we've heard about:

- Security programs that seem to work successfully in their business environments, even though they're run largely on instinct or experience rather than as formalized processes that could be extended into new areas.
- Security practitioners who feel like outsiders in the enterprise, because they're only called in when they're "needed" – when something's gone wrong – not before.
- Security managers who spend all their time performing tactical functions – responding to incidents, implementing password controls, installing and monitoring video or access systems – instead of developing strategies.
- Security programs that fail because they don't have the participation and support that they need from the rest of the enterprise.

- Security managers who are "blindsided" by security problems they weren't even aware existed – but are still expected to take the blame for.

There's a lot wrong here, and we'll be talking throughout this book about exactly what makes these things wrong and what you, as the security practitioner, can do about it. But for now, we'd like to talk about one key component that's missing from all these scenarios: consistency. In ESRM terms, consistency has two fundamental meanings:

1. Consistency in applying a security risk management philosophy to every part of the security function and to the thought processes applied to all security decision-making.
2. Consistency in how security roles and responsibilities are communicated to, and understood by, the internal strategic partners who are so critical to the success of an ESRM program.

Bringing consistency to your security program is essential to ensuring that all your stakeholders across the enterprise understand exactly what to expect from you as a security professional and from your security program, recognize and appreciate security's roles in the enterprise and its business value, and rely on you and your team to perform your roles as trusted business partners.

Consistency is driven by:

- Following known, documented, well communicated, practices.
- Remembering the proper steps of all security activities and processes.
- Always understanding the true role of the security professional as manager of security risk.
- Incorporating that understanding and philosophy into your everyday thought processes as the security manager.

Consistency in your security program offers many benefits, but none is more important than earning the trust of the business. When your strategic partners in the enterprise can see that you perform all your security work in a consistent manner and treat all aspects of security risk with a consistent approach, they'll understand that they can rely on you to practice your security discipline in a balanced way with their best interests in mind. This is a key advantage that practicing security in the ESRM model will bring.

## 1.3 What is ESRM? – A Closer Look

Let's take a closer look at exactly what ESRM is, and what it means for you as a security practitioner, and for everyone else impacted by this world of new and rapidly changing risks we all live in. And let's begin by building on the basic definition of ESRM that we've already offered:

> **Enterprise security risk management is the application of fundamental risk principles to manage all security risks – whether information, cyber, physical security, asset management, investigations, or business continuity – in a comprehensive, holistic, all-encompassing approach.**

What does this mean in practice? It means that ESRM represents a fundamental change in the way enterprises – and organizations and individuals within those enterprises – conduct some of their most business-critical operations. That takes time, commitment, and above all a process: an ongoing life cycle.

The ESRM life cycle is similar to other risk management cycles that you may already be familiar with such as the following:

- The International Organization for Standardization/International Electrotechnical Commission (ISO/IEC) risk management cycle, for example, calls for risks to be identified, analyzed, treated, and monitored (2009).
- The US Department of Commerce's National Institute of Standards and Technology (NIST) outlines a risk cycle – specific to cybersecurity and information security – in its *Guide for Conducting Risk Assessments* (2012) that calls for assessing risk, responding to it, and monitoring the results.
- The COBIT 5 model from the international professional association ISACA has a very similar implementation life cycle that includes recognizing needs (risks, in other words), defining desired state (planning mitigations) and monitoring outcomes (ongoing risk assessment).

As we've already explained, most of the basic, underlying concepts of ESRM are not new, and these other models have distinct similarities to ESRM. But the ESRM model has differences – differences that are critically important to security practitioners and to how they can run their security programs more effectively.

### 1.3.1 The Phases of the ESRM Life Cycle

In section 4 of this book, we'll do a deep exploration of all of the phases of the ESRM life cycle, but let's take a quick look at the model in Figure 1-1 to give you an idea of what we mean.

- **Identify and prioritize assets:** Identifying, understanding, and prioritizing the assets of an organization that need protection.
- **Identify and prioritize risks:** Identifying, understanding, and prioritizing the security threats the enterprise and its assets face – both existing and emerging – and, critically, the impacts and exposures associated with those threats.
- **Mitigate prioritized risks:** Taking the necessary, appropriate, and

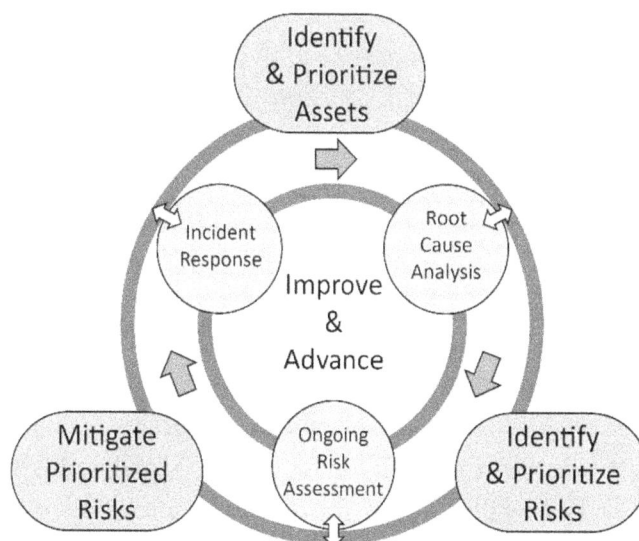

*Figure 1-1. The ESRM Cycle*

7

realistic steps to protect against the most serious security threats and risks.

- **Improve and advance:** Conducting incident response and review – learning from both successes and failures – and applying the lessons learned to advance the program.

This is a life cycle, but not necessarily a linear one. All of these functions are critical to protecting the enterprise – and all of them must be conducted simultaneously and on an ongoing basis. (That's why they're shown as a circle in our diagram.) Even more important, the ESRM life cycle requires ongoing commitment, not only from the security practitioner and the security organization, but also from stakeholders throughout the enterprise. It's only with that commitment, and thorough, consistent application across the enterprise, that ESRM can deliver on its true promise to protect the business and its assets.

### 1.3.2 Managing Risk in a Life Cycle

Part of applying the ESRM model – and one of the ways it differs from other models – is that the cycle requires you, as a security practitioner, to manage security risks both proactively and reactively. ASIS International's CSO Roundtable group (2015) published some of the earliest papers on the topic of ESRM, stressing this same idea that ESRM is:

- **Proactive** – continuously assess the full scope of security-related risks to protected assets.
- **Reactive** – respond to security incidents, mitigate the impact, and then assess residual risk to minimize exposure to recurrence, while learning how a risk may have changed and could affect the risk assessment progress and thinking all over again.

ESRM is a simple yet powerful management practice that enables the security professional to engage with the business, partner with the business, and guide the business through a comprehensive security risk management and security risk decision-making process. This enables the security professional and the strategic partner in the organization to work together to develop security strategy and accept risks that are acceptable to the business.

It's almost impossible to overstate the importance of that last phrase: acceptable to the business. Security and risk decisions must always be fully aligned with the needs and the objectives of the business, so that the business – not the security organization – can make sound, informed security risk decisions. Security practitioners don't always fully recognize that businesses need to take risks to be successful. ESRM principles can help the business take advantage of these risks, and can actually add real value to the business by doing so.

### 1.4 What ESRM Is – and What It Is Not

To truly succeed, every business function needs to fully understand why it exists and what it needs to do for the business it operates in, and security is no exception. (Make no mistake, security is a business function too, and your success depends on your recognizing that fact.) The ESRM philosophy provides a simple, effective way to frame the mission and goals of the security organization – for ourselves as security practitioners, for the people in our security organizations working to achieve those goals, and for business leaders. Let's begin by defining them for our own purposes.

## 1.4.1 ESRM Mission and Goals

As we mentioned before, the CSO Roundtable published an early description of ESRM in 2015. In it, they offered a simple, actionable definition of these concepts:

- The mission of ESRM is to identify, evaluate, and mitigate the impact of security risks to the business, with prioritized protective activities that enable the business to advance its overall mission.
- The goals of ESRM are to engage with the business to establish organizational policies, standards, and procedures to identify and manage security risks to the enterprise.

There's nothing terribly difficult for the security practitioner to understand about any of this. Essentially, when we embrace the ESRM philosophy, we want the business to help us identify what they need to have protected and what they care about, so that we can then assist them and provide input to make the right decisions to protect their assets and their business. But implementing ESRM – getting the business to understand, accept, and care about ESRM principles – is a very different matter.

Making the business understand that it's in their best interests to partner with security in identifying and mitigating risks is central to ESRM, and to your success as a security practitioner. And the mission-critical process of building that understanding and partnership is a theme that we'll keep returning to throughout this book.

While it might seem a bit counterintuitive, part of that process will be helping the business to understand what ESRM *is not*. There are a lot of different security and risk approaches out there, many of them well known and widely practiced. And when you're working to understand ESRM, and communicate its principles to others, it's very important that you first understand how and why it's different from those other approaches.

**Enterprise Security Risk Management vs. Enterprise Risk Management.** One common source of confusion about enterprise security risk management (ESRM) is its resemblance – at least in its name and its acronym – to a more general business and finance concept: enterprise risk management (ERM). ESRM is not the same as ERM, and it certainly doesn't replace it. As you work to communicate ESRM principles to business leaders, you may find you have to explain the fundamental difference. And the place to start, of course, is by understanding what ERM is. As we already mentioned, there are other risk models that you and your strategic partners might be familiar with, and it's important to understand that while similar, ESRM is not the same as these ERM models.

"Enterprise risk management (ERM) looks at the universe of risks – financial, strategic, accidental, and so on – that an organization faces. However, ERM doesn't always fully take into account the risks that are traditionally associated with security. Enterprise security risk management (ESRM) is a working philosophy ensuring that these risks are properly considered and treated." (CSO Roundtable of ASIS International, 2010)

ERM is often an established program or function within the enterprise, designed to manage risks for the business. These risks are not, by any means, limited to security risks. They may include literally any type of risk the enterprise could face – everything from market capitalization problems to the possibility of a hostile takeover. An ERM program usually has a defined scope, and often has a dedicated organization as well. ERM, like ESRM, uses risk principles when managing enterprise risks, which of course include, though they are not limited to, security risks. The security organization should always play a role in the ERM program – along with other functions, such as finance, human resources (HR), legal, and operations – to identify and address the security-related risks the enterprise may be facing.

ESRM uses risk management principles to manage any and all security-specific risks across an enterprise. It doesn't define a structure or program, but simply establishes a management process the security organization can use to guide the business in identifying, managing, and accepting security risks.

## 1.4.1.1 Enterprise Risk Management: A Brief Overview

The ERM concept was developed, defined, and codified by the financial services industry. Unsurprisingly, it focuses primarily on business and specifically on financial risks and activities. The original driver of ERM was the Committee of Sponsoring Organizations of the Treadway Commission (COSO). COSO is a joint initiative of five major professional associations: the American Accounting Association (AAA), the American Institute of Certified Public Accountants (AICPA), Financial Executives International (FEI), the Institute of Internal Auditors (IIA), and the National Association of Accountants (now the Institute of Management Accountants [IMA]). The Treadway Commission also included representatives from industry, public accounting, investment firms, and the New York Stock Exchange.

COSO defines ERM as follows:

> Enterprise risk management is a process, effected by an entity's board of directors, management and other personnel, applied in strategy setting and across the enterprise, designed to identify potential events that may affect the entity, and manage risk to be within its risk appetite, to provide reasonable assurance regarding the achievement of entity objectives. (Committee of Sponsoring Organizations of the Treadway Commission, 2004, p. 2)

So, what are the most important things you, as a security professional, need to know about ERM in order to understand the similarities to and differences from ESRM (and to explain to your strategic partners why one is not the other)? Again – based on what COSO wrote in 2004 about ERM:

- **ERM is a formal program.** ERM is an ongoing cycle, not simply a one-time action. Risk management never stops, because risk – every kind of risk – never stops. One risk might diminish as another increases, one might disappear entirely as business objectives change and introduce other, entirely different risks. It's the responsibility of the risk manager to continually scan the environment for risks and opportunities for the business. And that's something that can only be done through a defined and formalized program.
- **ERM is a group activity.** People at every level of the enterprise, from the board of directors to frontline personnel, must be aware of the business environment and objectives, and understand how their activities can have a positive or negative impact on the business.
- **ERM applies at both the strategic and operational level, across the entire enterprise.** Every part of the enterprise, without exception, has some degree of exposure to some kind of risk. ERM takes a holistic view of the business and understand the whole business in order to manage risk with a broad view (Committee of Sponsoring Organizations of the Treadway Commission, 2004, p. 2).

While COSO's is just one of several industry frameworks for ERM, for the security practitioner's purposes – and especially for use in communicating with business leaders – the COSO definition is a particularly useful one.

Table 1-1 below shows some of the significant differences between ERM and ESRM that you should be aware of.

**Table 1-1: What is the Difference Between ERM and ESRM?**

| Enterprise Risk Management | Enterprise Security Risk Management |
|---|---|
| Focuses on all aspects of organizational risk – operational, environmental, and especially financial. | Focuses solely on managing security risks to organization assets. |
| Is a defined program with specific structure, usually a department in and of itself. | Is a working philosophy of managing security risk through traditional risk management principals, but doesn't require any particular department structure. |
| Programs may or may not include/look at security related risks as part of the overall risk profile of the organization. | Doesn't look for risks outside the security realm. |

So we've established that ERM and ESRM are very different, approaching a different set of issues in different ways. The principal difference is that ERM is a function, typically a department, while ESRM is a working philosophy for dealing with one kind of risk – security. Despite their differences, they do have one very important principle in common:

> **They both use traditional risk principles to manage the risk process**, and those risk principles apply to many risk management issues, extending beyond both ERM and ESRM.

## 1.4.2 ESRM vs. Security Organization Convergence

Another recent shift in the risk conversation among security professionals (that is actually very different in its goals and in its approach from ESRM) is *security organization convergence.*

Oftentimes we'll see discussions about *security risk management* that are simply advocating having a single job or department responsible for both logical (information technology or IT) and physical security tasks. Security *convergence* is an organization model combining the management of physical and logical security departments under one leadership umbrella to manage all the security risks. ESRM, as we've already explained, is a holistic working philosophy of security, while the convergence discussion is a much more limited one, centering on enterprise organizational, task, and personnel structures.

Convergence became a hot issue in the 1990s, when the significance of information security threats began to become clear, and gathered impetus in the early part of the 21st century. In response to increasing threats and risks around computer systems and data, security professionals began to focus on what they saw as the need to combine the organizational structures of the physical security and information security departments for power, efficiency, and consistency purposes. According to Ray Bernard (2011) in an article on convergence, "In leading organizations, the union between corporate and physical security and IT is established around key touch points, with increasing collaboration under an overall objective to benefit from convergence that is followed up by specific planning." But there is no focus on risk-based management in the overall convergence discussion.

It is possible that implementing ESRM, as a philosophy and a program, may eventually lead to convergence in security leadership, due simply to synergistic philosophies and management requirements. But we want to be clear – *security organization convergence is not one of the goals of ESRM.* ESRM is not concerned at its core with the personnel structure of the departments tasked with security activities that mitigate risks – whether those risks are logical or physical. And convergence, the concept of a department structure that combines task management of both logical and physical security tasks, is a separate conversation. Under ESRM, the fundamental role of all types of security practitioners and managers, no matter their department structure, is to manage all the types of security risks using the same risk principles and with a common strategy.

The discussion in the security community about various benefits of, and approaches to, converging the information security and physical security departments is ongoing. The practice and philosophy of ESRM doesn't address the actual organizational structure of the security function, because ESRM is a philosophical approach to managing all security risks, no matter the asset, the threat, or the function, and it applies to both physical and information security. No matter which side of the convergence discussion you are on, though, convergence is certainly a force for change in the overall security conversation – but not required by the ESRM philosophy. If, however, your organization does decide to converge the two areas into a single functional structure, we believe that the only way to find true success in managing that converged security model would be through a well-defined and implemented ESRM program.

Table 1-2 below shows some of the significant differences between security organization convergence and ESRM that you should be aware of.

**Table 1-2. What is the Difference Between Security Organization Convergence and ESRM?**

| Security Organization Convergence | Enterprise Security Risk Management |
|---|---|
| Specifically calls for an organization structure that manages all security tasks – logical and physical – under a single management structure. | Doesn't recommend any particular management structure, but does require that all security risks be treated with its principles. |
| Is concerned with determining whether a risk is specific to IT vs. all other types of security. | Treats all security risk the same and prioritizes risks according to potential impact to assets. |

# 2

# Why Does the Security Industry Need ESRM?

Simply put, security professionals, and the security industry as a whole, need ESRM to address many issues that security practitioners face every day in attempting to accomplish the daunting task of securing the people and assets of an enterprise in the face of a continually evolving and increasingly risky global security landscape.

Here we'll explore a number of the typical frustrations, issues, and problems we've seen in our own careers, and heard from in the stories of our peers in the security profession. ESRM is the solution to those problems – as we'll argue, and hope you'll see, over the course of this book.

## 2.1 Why Does the Traditional Approach to Security Frustrate So Many People?

One of the most critical issues we've found in our discussions with our peers in the security profession, and with their strategic partners inside their organizations, is that almost everyone involved with security (whether the practitioner or the impacted stakeholder) often experiences a sense of frustration at the process and the experience. This frustration can manifest in many different ways, whether the security practitioner becomes frustrated that an internal business partner has overturned or dismissed a security proposal, or has had the security requirements dictated to them against their recommendation, or a business leader is frustrated that security requirements are onerous and interfering with getting their work done (to name just a few).

When we looked at all of the various frustrations, however, we found that they are often the result of one of two things:

- The security practitioner is not fully aware of what his or her role is.
- The strategic partner is not fully aware of what security's role is.

Both of these situations are avoidable – and are the responsibility of the security practitioner to correct: first, by clearly and completely understanding the role of the security function in the overall enterprise as mangers of security risk; and, second, by communicating to the strategic partner a comprehensive understanding of that role and appropriately setting the expectations of what the security practitioner and the strategic partner should be doing in the security risk management process.

Now we'll take a look at this familiar issue – from the perspective of both the security practitioner and a business function leader – in a story that is fictional, but is something that happens in real life all too often. Moving on, we'll examine a security risk and incident as played out in the "traditional" security environment.

### 2.1.1 The Missing Network Switch: A Story of Security Frustration in a Traditional Security Environment

#### *The Security Practitioner's Story*

Rick is a security manager for Aspect Insurance, a multibillion-dollar health insurance provider. He has been assigned the task of protecting one of his company's data centers, which is undergoing a major upgrade involving an independent contractor. Data security is a business-critical concern for the company because its operations are subject to rigorous regulatory compliance requirements, including the strictures of the Health Insurance Portability and Accountability Act (HIPAA). The data center handles massive amounts of personally identifiable information, including medical records, claims data, credit card numbers, and other financial data. A security breach would be a disaster, exposing the company to regulatory scrutiny, legal liability, and serious reputational damage to its brand.

Rick knows all this, and he is concerned about the security risks associated with having outside contractors working in such a sensitive location. In keeping with established industry best practices, he recommends conducting background checks for all of the contract employees involved in the project. But when the data center's facility and finance managers see the plan, they are not convinced that it's either necessary or worth the cost – which is not covered in the project budget and would require that they find new funding. They also don't see the issue as "their problem." To them, data security is somebody else's concern. They know that because of the sensitivity of the data, the IT group has implemented strong intrusion detection and prevention technologies. The facility and finance managers point to the security measures that are already in place – including physical ones in the general facility like video cameras and card readers – and don't see the need for more. And so they reject Rick's recommendations.

Rick comes away from his presentation feeling that his expertise is not being valued and that he is not being allowed to do what he was hired to do: protect the company. More importantly, he comes away deeply concerned about the security of the data center – and it doesn't take long for his worst fears to be realized. Three months after his presentation, a network switch is stolen from a server rack in the data center by a contracted employee who, it later comes to light, has burglary convictions on his record. The hardware is valued at only a few thousand dollars, but in the course of the theft, several active servers are badly damaged and months' worth of critical data has been compromised. The data might have been destroyed as part of the theft, or possibly copied, stolen, and corrupted using the theft as an attempt to hide the data as the target. And all the elaborate cybersecurity measures the company had put into place were meaningless, because someone simply walked into the data center with a malicious intention.

When he learns of the incident, Rick has an "I told you so!" moment. (Of course, as a professional, he keeps it to himself.) But it doesn't last long, because he, as the security manager, is the one who is held responsible for letting the intrusion happen. He begins an investigation that quickly identifies an employee of the independent contractor who was onsite at the time as the likely thief. But by that time, the employee had quit working for the contractor and was gone. And in any case, Rick now has a far more important problem: putting together an emergency project to implement protections – essentially the same protections he recommended months ago.

### The Business Function Leader

Paul K. is the network and systems vice president responsible for the systems that were damaged in the theft of the network card. His team is under intense pressure to repair the damage, get the servers back up and running, determine whether the data was destroyed (which would be a bad outcome) or actually stolen (which would be even worse), and discover whether any of the compromised data was personally identifiable information or health-record data. If he can't definitively establish that the data was not stolen, he'll have to begin the reporting process for a potential HIPPA violation. And all the time this is going on, he has to restore regular business operations including recovering the lost data, some of which was not backed up yet and will have to be re-created from scratch. Angry at what he sees as a clear security failure, Paul calls Rick in and demands to know what went wrong and why.

Rick explains that the theft could have been prevented if the background checks he recommended – that were rejected because they were too expensive – had been in place. Instead of being appeased by this, Paul is now angrier than ever. He feels Rick should have fought harder for the security controls he believed were necessary – and that, by not fighting harder for those controls, he has not done his job. Rick was tasked with protecting the data center, and from Paul's perspective, he obviously did not do that.

At the end of our story, both Rick and Paul – the security practitioner and the strategic partner – are unhappy and frustrated at the security organization's seeming inability to "get things done." And the main reason for their frustration, and for the security failure that brought it to a head, is a fundamental and very common situation: a security professional given the responsibility to undertake an assignment, but not the authority to carry it out.

These problems – both the security failure and the frustration and "blame game" that go along with them – could have been prevented by the application of ESRM principles and an understanding by all parties of security's role throughout the process. Next, we'll take a look at how this situation might have played out in a company, and a security organization, that based its decision on the ESRM philosophy.

## 2.1.2 The Missing Network Switch: A Story of Security Partnership in an ESRM Security Environment

### The Security Practitioner

When Rick is tasked with protecting the data center, he views the assignment not simply as a security problem to be solved, but as a security risk issue to be managed. He begins by identifying the serious risks – regulatory, legal, and reputational – the company would face in the event of a security failure during the data center upgrade. Then he identifies the key stakeholders who would be impacted by a security failure, and realizes they include an extraordinarily broad range of roles and organizations in the company. And for that reason, instead of allowing his recommendations for background checks on all of the independent contractors' employers to be rejected by the facility manager, Rick goes to where he believes the risk "lives": First to Paul, the network and systems vice president, then also to the general counsel, who would own the regulatory risk.

### *The Business Function Leader*

At first, Paul doesn't understand why Rick has come to him about background checks, when the facility manager and finance manager have already rejected the proposal as too expensive. But when Rick lays out in detail the possible consequences of a security failure, he sees that the risks would, in fact, directly impact him, far more than they would impact either facilities or finance. He decides that the risks are unacceptable to his network and data security, and that the costs of background checks are small compared to his data security risks. He brings in the human resources (HR) and legal departments, and asks Rick to collaborate with them in designing and conducting background checks on all of the independent contractor's employees assigned to the project. Rick and Paul are both satisfied: Paul because his risk is mitigated, and Rick because the risk mitigation decision was made by the correct risk owner.

### 2.1.3 The Missing Network Switch: Lessons Learned and the ESRM Difference

Our scenario, as we left it above, could have two different endings:

1. The background checks could reveal that several of the employees the contractor was planning to have onsite in the data center have misrepresented their employment histories, some have exaggerated their technical qualifications, and one actually has an extensive criminal record. The contractor would immediately remove those employees from the project, and the network switch would never be stolen, because the thief is never allowed into the data center.
2. Events could played out differently. Paul might listen, understand the risk, and still choose not to accept the additional project costs of background checks, and the theft and damage might still occur.

Crucially, though, with ESRM principles in place:

- The responsibility for the security risk would have resided in the appropriate place: with the owner of the business assets at risk.
- Paul, as the business owner, would have been faced with accepting the residual risk from that business-critical decision. (If he did, Rick might even have made the very difficult decision to go over his head and take his concerns to a higher level in the company.)
- It would have been difficult, if not impossible, for anyone to lay the blame on Rick or the security organization, because it was clear that it was Paul who owned the risk and that both Rick and Paul had followed a thoughtful security risk decision-making process.

This fundamental concept – the acceptance of risk by its true owner – is an essential component of ESRM.

As security professionals, we know that security incidents are always going to happen. Information assets will be lost, physical assets will be stolen or damaged, and business processes will be interrupted. There is no such thing as perfect security, and there never will be. However, we believe that when security professionals are not practicing ESRM as the basis of their security program, the wrong people can often be making security and risk decisions, whether based on right information and criteria or not. Most often we see that they are the wrong decision-makers, not because they should have no say in the decision, but because they are not the sole asset owner or stakeholder, and they should not have the only say. Sometimes, as we saw in the example above of a function making a security decision solely on a financial basis, the decision-maker is not a true stakeholder in the risk at all. And when things go wrong, as they inevitably will, it's the security professional who will take the blame, mostly because they, or their partners in the organization, did not have a clearly defined understanding of what the security practitioner's role was in the first place.

It may not be fair, but it's the reality that most security professionals live with every day, and it can, and does, cause frustration for the security practitioner and strategic partner alike. And yet, it doesn't have to be. As we'll show you through the course of this book, ESRM principles can significantly reduce the number of stories like Rick and Paul's. And one of the most important ways ESRM can do that is by shifting the security practitioner's focus from daily task management to strategic risk management. Practicing ESRM will make the day-to-day and career of a security professional more satisfying.

## 2.2 What Do We Mean by "Traditional" Security vs. ESRM?

As we move through this book, we'll discuss the concepts of "traditional" security, as compared to the enterprise security risk management philosophy. Before we go any further, though, we want to walk through a few scenarios that clarify what we mean by "traditional" security, so you have a basis of understanding of what we are moving away from, as we move toward a risk-based security approach.

### 2.2.1 What Does Security Do? The Traditional View

Here's an exercise that we think you'll find is an eye-opener. The next time you're in a room full of security professionals, try asking this deceptively simple question: *What does security do?*

#### 2.2.1.1 The Answer from the Security Practitioner

Chances are, you'll get as many different responses as there are people in the room. During the discussion, here are a few of the comments you're likely to hear:

- Security's job is to protect the company's business assets.

- Information security – making sure sensitive personal information, like credit card data, is protected.
- We're focused on physical security.
- Investigating breaches of company security policy.

These responses aren't wrong, exactly – especially not from the point of view of the individual who's been asked the question. In fact, from the perspective of the traditional way of approaching security, they're essentially correct. And that's the heart of the problem. The answers are all very different, they're all incomplete, and some, like the one about security investigating security breaches, actually seem to go around in circles. We as security professionals need to have our own ideas straight before we can begin to communicate them to others. And as you'll see, communication is one of the most important elements of ESRM.

### 2.2.1.2 The Answer from the Board of Directors and Senior Executives

Now let's say you left that room full of security people and walked next door to ask the same question to a group of board members, line-of-business owners, or senior executives. You'd almost certainly get an equally wide-ranging, equally "correct" – and equally incomplete and inadequate – set of answers. We suspect that in trying to define the role of security, the discussion would include some things like this:

- Security manages the physical security on our property, like the guards and gates.
- Security protects our data – through things like password management and network monitoring.
- It is all about protecting our people on campus – and making sure our systems and data are safe.
- They help keep us up and running if something goes really wrong, like a natural disaster.

Those responses aren't wrong, either. They're based on these key decision-makers' perceptions, their perspectives, and their experiences. But, just like the security practitioners' responses, they're incomplete – no longer adequate to define what security is – if they ever were. And that's important, because if we can't define security, we can't possibly be sure we're getting it right. Once again, ESRM enables us to easily define what it is security does, how we do it, and how it helps the whole organization. It goes beyond what we see in both sets of answers above that are simply describing the tasks we're responsible for, to defining security's true role in the enterprise.

### 2.2.1.3 The Answer from Operational Personnel

Another walk down the hall might be even more revealing. Walk into just about any location – the HR department, the factory floor, research and development (R&D), wherever – and you may not even have to ask any questions. You may see operational personnel exchange nervous glances; somebody may make an uneasy joke along the lines of "Uh-oh, we're in trouble now!"; or a manager may come up and ask "What's wrong?" in a tone that suggests you're about to shut down his operation to deal with some security problem.

But why? Why do so many of the people we're trying to protect see us as a nuisance, or as a problem, or possibly even as the enemy? Well, one very important reason is that most of us, traditionally, only interact with operational personnel (the managers and employees who keep the business running) in an enforcement role, when we're responding to some kind of security incident. When we follow ESRM principles, we'll instead build constructive working relationships with people in a broad range of roles across the enterprise, explaining what we do and learning what they do. And though it might seem hard to believe right now, the result is that they are sometimes actually glad to see us come through the door.

## 2.2.2 Why the Security Industry Needs to Define "Security"

Reactions like the ones we've walked through above clearly don't reflect a comprehensive, accurate view of the important work you do – and they certainly don't reflect the way you want yourself and your role to be perceived. But they're all too common, and they're highly damaging to your effectiveness and your success as a security professional.

That's why defining security – our role, our objectives, and our way of measuring success – is so important. If we can't define what we do, how we do it, and why we do it, we can't possibly be sure we're successful. And we can't ensure that security is recognized as the serious professional business discipline that it needs to be. We'll be leaving it to others to define security through their perceptions and experiences, and define them in ways that we aren't likely to agree with.

One of the reasons this is such a critical problem is that letting people outside of security define what security does often results in the security practice within an enterprise being broken up, or "siloed," with physical security responsibilities handled separately from information security and cybersecurity responsibilities and sometimes even some security activities being handled by groups outside of security entirely, such as HR or audit performing investigations or facilities handling guard services.

We often work in "siloed" organizations because we've never clearly defined what security's role is in the business environment. Instead, because we *as an industry* haven't clearly defined security's role, it has been left up to others to define it for us – and, inevitably, that means that "security's role" is seen as strictly the specific tasks assigned to us, and any attempt to discuss aspects of security outside of those tasks is seen as overreaching our role. That isn't good for security as a professional discipline, isn't good for our careers, and most importantly, isn't good for the security of the enterprises we work for. But it doesn't have to be this way.

So you may well ask: If it doesn't have to be this way, why do security practitioners, business executives, operational managers, and ordinary employees still have so many different answers to the question of what security is, and such different expectations of what the security department should be doing? And also, how is ESRM's definition different?

The answer lies in several problems we'll be discussing in this book:

- The absence of a consistent "philosophy" of security management.

- A focus on tactical functions – daily operational tasks – rather than strategic, risk-focused, decision-making, that leads to our programs being defined by those functions and assigned tasks.
- A view of the security practitioner's role that centers on enforcement of rules, rather than on management of risks.
- The desire to keep potential problems from coming to light, in order to "protect" the security organization, when facing them head-on would ultimately be better for both the organization and the business as a whole.

All of these problems can lead to weakened security that can compromise the business, and lead to frustration – and serious professional and career problems – for both security practitioners and their strategic partners in the organization. And they can be addressed, mostly effectively, by the application of ESRM principles.

### 2.2.3 What Does Security Do? The ESRM View

In this book, we'll be taking a close look at that same deceptively simple question: ***What does security do?***

And then we'll be going even deeper, into mission-critical issues like:

- What is the security practitioner's and the security organization's role in the business?
- How can security practitioners manage their thought processes throughout their daily practices to best serve the organizations they work in?

We'll share the lessons we've learned in our many years as security professionals; we'll share some of the answers we've come up with to the questions we've raised; and, more importantly, we'll give you a framework for coming up with answers on your own.

The widely varying responses and reactions from security practitioners, businesspeople, and employees when they were asked to define security suggest that it's a difficult question; but it really isn't, when ESRM principles are applied. ESRM offers a very simple, highly definitive, and extremely useful answer:

***Security manages the enterprise's security risks through the use of basic risk principles.***

Remember our roomful of security professionals? Whether they recognize it or not, their responses to the question "What does security do?" can all be distilled down to "We manage security risks." Take a look at the comparison in Table 2-1 to see what their statements really mean, when they're looked at through the lens of ESRM. The bottom line is: Security's role is managing security risks using fundamental risk principles.

**Table 2-1. Views of Security Through an ESRM Lens**

| The Task-Based View of Security | The ESRM View of Security |
|---|---|
| *Security's job is to protect the company's business assets.* | To be precise, security means protecting all of the company's assets – physical, logical, and human – against the many risks presented by a fast-changing and increasingly dangerous world. All the security measures we take, from video cameras at building entrances to the most sophisticated anti-malware systems, are aimed at managing and mitigating known and emerging risks. |
| *Information security – making sure sensitive personal information, like credit card numbers, is protected.* | A seemingly endless series of high-profile data security breaches, from WikiLeaks' release of sensitive US military and intelligence files to the Ashley Madison hack, shows the risks of inadequate information security – risks that can literally be fatal for a company. ESRM principles recognize the range of security risks, and help security professionals and their strategic partners in the enterprise address them appropriately while understanding each other's roles in the management process. |
| *We're focused on physical security.* | Physical security is the practice of protecting the company's physical property from a variety of security risks, ranging from theft to damage to misuse. The ESRM approach, however, views this as an aspect of risk – a mitigation plan to reduce exposure and impact. A theft by an employee, for example, might be seen as a minor infraction of company policy – but it could have a serious impact on asset protection if it's not dealt with effectively from the beginning. |
| *Investigating breaches of company security policy.* | When security policies are not followed, whether intentionally or unintentionally, the company is exposed to an enormous range of risks, ranging for legal liability to fines for regulatory noncompliance to reputational and brand damage. Investigation is the first, necessary response to an indication of a breach of policy, and, more importantly, the first step in understanding root causes and mitigating the risk(s) involved. |

## 2.2.3.1 Managing Security Risks

In our examples so far, we only scratched the surface of the many different types of security risks you may be responsible for related to the different tasks you may need to undertake to manage and mitigate those risks. There are many, many more risks and tasks to deal with that exist across multiple disciplines such as:

- Investigations.
- Physical security.
- Cyber and information security.
- Workplace violence and threat management.
- Business continuity and crisis management.

For now, though, what matters most is that we recognize that the specific tasks security performs that mitigate risks don't define *security* and don't truly describe the profession nor the role of the security professional. They are all parts of our responsibilities as security practitioners, but they don't even come close to representing the entirety of what we do, what we need to do, and what we need to be recognized as doing.

Managing security risks enterprise-wide – and managing the process of managing security risks in partnership with business leaders enterprise-wide – is your role and your responsibility as a security professional. And ESRM, because it's comprehensive, holistic, and all-encompassing, is what makes that possible.

Unfortunately, we continue to see the tasks of the security discipline presented – in books, in articles, in conference presentations, in interactions with our colleagues and our industry peers – as defining what security is and what security does. We routinely hear, for example, how security manages video surveillance, guards, firewall administration, or password control. But we don't hear how those tasks tie to the role of the department, or how they and the practitioners fit into a consistent philosophy or methodology of security. And we believe this approach to defining security is fundamentally wrong, and fundamentally dangerous.

Why is it so important for us to define what we as security professionals do as "managing security risk," rather than simply listing tasks and responsibilities? It is because, no matter what type of security risk is being discussed, the practice of managing those security risks is essentially the same. That means we're completely consistent in our approach to, execution of, and messaging about the security program. And describing what we do as managing security risks closes awareness gaps on how we are perceived by our peers inside the organization, makes it easier for others to understand what we do, and more willing to partner with us in protecting the enterprise.

### 2.2.3.2 Basic Risk Principles
The definition of ESRM states that security risks are managed through risk principles. But what, exactly, does that mean? There are well-established, fundamental risk principles – principles that have been tested and found effective over many years, in many different enterprises, and in many different industries – that can be used to manage risks of all types.

We encourage you to explore risk management standards and documents to gain greater insight into the topic of basic risk principles.

Here is a short (non-exhaustive) list of risk management standards to consider:

- Carnegie Mellon Operationally Critical Threat, Asset, and Vulnerability Evaluation (OCTAVE).
- European Union Agency for Network and Information Security (ENISA) Risk Management/Risk Assessment (RM/RA) Framework.
- National Institute of Standards and Technology (NIST) Cybersecurity Framework.
- ISACA Control Objectives for Information and Related Technology (COBIT 5) framework.
- International Organization for Standardization (ISO) Enterprise Risk Management model.

## 2.3 The Security Professional and the Business Leader: Moving Beyond Frustration with One Another

We've already discussed how frustrating it can be when the business doesn't accept our decisions, our recommendations, or the plans we're trying to implement. And we've acknowledged that security can be every bit as frustrating for business leaders, who often see security as a costly obstacle to getting things done. Part of the problem, of course, is that business leaders don't necessarily recognize the importance of what we do, and what we're trying to do. To put the problem in its simplest terms, they don't recognize what our role in the enterprise is.

But that doesn't mean all the responsibility for understanding roles lies with the other business leaders in your organization. We, as security professionals and leaders, also have a responsibility to recognize what our role is, and what it is not. At its most basic, our security role of managing security risk means guiding the business through the decision-making process – not making the decisions ourselves. It's very important that we as security practitioners recognize that this isn't avoiding responsibility or "passing the buck" in any way. When it comes to security, in the broadest sense, we're the subject-matter experts, and we're the people the business should be looking to for strategic insight and tactical guidance on risk decisions. But in an ESRM environment, our increasing value as security practitioners – and, also importantly, our increasing personal and professional satisfaction – comes from guiding our strategic partners in the organization through a proper decision-making process about the risks to the business assets they own.

Now, there are clearly two sides to this process:

1. Helping the business understand security.
2. Helping security understand the business.

As a security professional, you can play a critical role in both parts, but the place to start is by working to understand what your enterprise wants and needs from you. And you can best do that by the simplest means possible: *by asking them.*

We think you'll find that your partners will appreciate the interest you take in what they do – and in many cases, we also think you'll find it's the first time anyone from security has ever asked these questions. Asking these questions and showing an interest in the business leaders who will become your strategic partners in the organization is the first step toward realizing the benefits that can accrue from using ESRM – the beginning of building effective partnerships that benefit everyone.

We'll further explore understanding your business environment in section 3 of this book, but for now, here are three simple questions to ask your business counterparts that will help you better understand the business, and your role in protecting it:

- What are the main objectives that you want to accomplish?
- What do you consider worth protecting?
- What do you care about most – and what do you care about the least?

These few questions, as simple as they are, are already leading you into the ESRM life cycle – the first phase of identifying the assets that need to be protected, then prioritizing them according to the business's priorities. The questions may seem obvious, especially to an experienced security professional, but you may find that the answers you get to them are not.

You may think, for example, that the enterprise's physical infrastructure is what matters most, but there may actually be intellectual property that's far more valuable to the business. Business leaders may be worried about the impact of a natural disaster or a pandemic on operational continuity, while you're focusing on malware or other aspects of IT security. Either of you may be thinking about emerging threats – for example, the reputational damage that can come from internal documents being leaked on social media, or potential instability in global supply chains resulting from local conflicts over water rights – that the other hasn't even considered.

As you develop a clearer understanding of the enterprise's business objectives, you may find the overall picture isn't quite as comprehensive or coherent as you thought. A certain project may, for example, deviate from the enterprise's overall business mission, and may present more, or less, risk. The security practitioner needs to help guide the relevant business stakeholders in developing a precise, granular understanding of risks and risks tolerances, to ensure that risk decisions are made by the right stakeholders at the right level and based on the right information.

Once we understand what business leaders want to protect – the human, physical, and intellectual assets they value most – it's much easier for us to help them recognize the risks to those assets. And, of course, it's also much easier for us to get them to accept the cost, whether in terms of budget or operational efficiency, of protections against those risks of harm to the assets they've already identified as important. That process of recognizing and prioritizing risk, transferring residual risk to the right stakeholders, and helping those stakeholders make appropriate security risk decisions, is the essence of ESRM. And the payoff for the security practitioners comes when the business recognizes the true value of security, and embraces it as something that adds real-world business value.

## 2.4 ESRM-Based Security: Moving from Task Management to Risk Management

At the heart of ESRM is the recognition that security is an overarching strategic concern, not a set of tactical, operational tasks to be performed. In order to move into the ESRM model of managing security, you'll need to shift your focus from managing daily tasks to managing strategic risks.

### 2.4.1 Task Management

In today's security world, every practitioner is busy, sometimes too busy to get all the things done they need to do, let alone take on any new programs. There are threats to monitor, video cameras to repair, investigations starting up, gates to guard, executives to protect, data to encrypt, metrics to analyze and report on, and employees to manage. So it's not surprising, as we saw earlier in our "questions" exercise, that the tasks we perform every day come to define our discipline to us and to others – and that they are the first things that come to mind when we are asked to explain what we do for the company. It is not surprising, but it's a mistake. It is a mistake that damages our effectiveness and credibility as security professionals and, even more important, compromises the security of the people and assets we are tasked with protecting.

Why? Because when you define your role as doing things, completing tasks, then it's easy for people to view that task as unimportant, or not their problem, or not something that should come out of their budget. It is just one task or item, after all. But ESRM can change that, by ensuring that security's role is clear, that you are seen as a manager of risks. Being seen as managing risks means, in turn, that those risks must at least be considered when security decisions are made, or else the decision-makers are not fulfilling their responsibility to perform due diligence on protecting their operations, or at a more basic level, even simply making educated security decisions about their assets.

### 2.4.2 Risk Management

Risk management, as we mentioned earlier, is the identification, assessment, treatment, and monitoring of security risks to the organization. It is fundamentally different from task management, because it means looking at ways to protect the company at a strategic level, as well as at a tactical level. It is deeply concerned with allowing the enterprise to complete its mission with minimal interruption from security-related incidents. Risk management can still involve tasks, but these are tasks with a higher purpose, tasks that are given to security personnel as a way to mitigate an identified risk. In this way, the role of the security group is to carry out a program that helps the company protect itself, not just to manage a gate or a guard or an access control method.

This may seem like playing with words, but in reality, this small difference in approach can lead to a very big change in the way security is perceived. We saw an example of that change earlier in our story of Rick performing background checks in the service of mitigating a risk of HIPAA violations and protecting valuable data center resources. Managing that risk and enacting a background check system decided upon and approved by the owner of the data center is different from just requiring checks because "security said so." After all, it's not the security organization that wants to avoid a HIPAA fine, it's the business as a whole.

## 2.5 The ESRM Solution: A New Philosophy

Implementing ESRM brings with it a holistic view of securing the enterprise through a consistent philosophy and management methodology. This view extends far beyond the day-to-day operational tasks that are assigned to the security organization. In fact, it extends beyond the narrower conception of security many of us are used to, because ESRM recognizes that security is always about managing risk, not just performing tasks.

It seems obvious, and yet, many security professionals assess risks and implement risk mitigation plans (in the form of the security tasks that they do on a daily basis) without considering that they are, in fact, aspects of overall, enterprise-wide security risk management. That lack of consideration of how the tasks impact overall risk means that moving from a task-oriented, performance-based security program to a comprehensive, holistic ESRM program requires a fundamental shift in the way security professionals think about both security and risk and how they think about how their current responsibilities fit in to the overarching role security needs to play in the enterprise. When we change the way we think, we change the way we present ourselves, and therefore we also change how others see us. That all comes in the application of the ESRM philosophy.

### 2.5.1 Security Becomes Strategic

What, exactly, is the ESRM philosophy? It revolves around identifying an asset at risk from harm and then identifying the possible impact of that risk; finding the owner(s) of that risk; developing and coordinating a risk mitigation strategy; responding to incidents; and learning from root causes about why an incident occurred and could occur again. This change in thought processes works over time to mature the functioning of the security organization, turning security managers into security and risk professionals. Just as importantly, it changes the perceptions of other stakeholders across the enterprise, from your internal business partners to senior executives to board members. And that means the difference between being seen as a tactical, operational problem-solver and – eventually – as a strategic partner.

### 2.5.2 Security Becomes a Business Function

Of course, we are not suggesting that security management *never* involves managing operational tasks or implementing security processes and systems. It always has, and it always will. But security task management becomes ESRM when those security processes and systems are put in place, enterprise-wide, according to a strategic framework developed with input from business function leaders.

Those leaders are the people with the most at stake in protecting those assets. They're the ones who must take responsibility for them; they're the ones who must decide on the value to the

28

enterprise of any risk mitigation plan. Now, the risk mitigation plan that's chosen will likely (but not always) be assigned to the security organization to implement and manage. But the plan itself will be the end result of a well-thought-out business decision.

Let's take another look at those last two words: business decision. It's almost impossible to overemphasize their importance, because they represent the critical difference between security management and ESRM. ESRM means ensuring that security is a business function based on a clear-eyed understanding of business risk. When we see security as a business function like any other – one that delivers real-world business benefits – our strategic partners will see it the same way.

We've run security organizations based on both the traditional and the ESRM models, and we've talked to many more security practitioners who've done it both ways. And we've come to the conclusion that ESRM is the best way forward for both the security professional and the strategic partners in the organization – and the best way to protect the enterprise.

## 2.6 ESRM as a Path to Security Success

In 2010, ASIS International's CSO Roundtable conducted a benchmarking study of security professionals and leaders to determine the extent to which ESRM concepts were being accepted in enterprises across the globe. A couple of quotes from the resulting white paper show that ESRM principles are very much top-of-mind for both security and business executives.
According to Timothy Williams, Director of Global Security, Caterpillar:

> With ESRM's holistic approach to security came the understanding that a whole host of business issues that were not traditionally associated with "security" – think, for example, of Sarbanes-Oxley or HIPAA – were now firmly part of security's bailiwick, underscoring again how important it's for security professionals to be business professionals first. (p. 3)

Dr. Erwann O. Michel-Kerjan, Managing Director, Risk Management and Decision Processes Center, The Wharton School of the University of Pennsylvania, explains:

> The growing recognition of Enterprise Security Risk Management (ESRM) as a holistic view of risk – all risks – throughout an organization is important; this holistic view helps ensure that the threats that might typically not be recognized in an enterprise risk management program focusing primarily on financial risks (such overlooked risks, for example, might include: risks to brand and reputation; physical supply-chain risks; or loss of consumer confidence if your data is stolen or networks attacked) are now more and more fully identified, prioritized, and mitigated. (p. 5)

These comments, and many others from security and business thought leaders, show an emerging consensus that ESRM is a must for security success – now, and as we move into an increasingly complex and dangerous future. And central to ESRM is the recognition that security success is simply business success.

As a security professional, you're operating in an environment driven, for the most part, by profit and value. This isn't the whole story, of course. There are government and nonprofit organizations, for example, that aren't profit-making entities, and even many private-sector businesses have goals other than profit (contributing to the wellbeing of their employees or their communities, for example). But most enterprises, certainly, are interested in protecting and increasing the value they deliver to their owners, their shareholders, their customers, and others. And every enterprise, whatever its mission, has a critical interest in protecting the assets it views as important. These two points come together in the ESRM philosophy, and understanding them and applying them is crucial to your success as a security professional.

## 2.6.1 What Does "Security Success" Look Like?

We all want our security efforts to be successful, and of course we all want to be successful in our security careers. But security success isn't necessarily easy to define, or even to recognize. That's a serious problem, because if we don't know what success looks like, we can never be sure we've achieved it. Try a simple thought experiment: You were suddenly put in charge of setting up a brand-new security program for your entire company. Now you're six months in, and the senior executives who gave you that responsibility want to know whether the program is a success. How will you determine how successful the program has been so far, and how will you communicate your conclusions to those high-level decision-makers?

### 2.6.1.1 Success Is Not Just Measured by Numbers

Maybe you'll look for key performance metrics. Those metrics could measure anything from the number of investigations your organization has conducted to the dollar value of the reduction in losses from fraud. They could represent the number of intrusion attempts that you've intercepted. Or maybe they'd show a reduction – or at least rationalization – of your security budget, as the right people with the right skill sets are assigned to the right tasks, and some previously manual tasks are automated.

Those are all great data points, and they're all useful, even necessary. But do any of those numbers, individually or in the aggregate, really define "success"? We don't think so. They're necessary, because they define scope, scale, efficiency, and effectiveness, which are all important, but they don't communicate whether a set risk tolerance threshold has changed in a way that would indicate a need to adapt. That's why, in this book, we'll present a new approach to defining the success of your security program – an approach based on ESRM principles.

### 2.6.1.2 In Security Success, Intangibles Are Important

ESRM success – not just security success – will be measured at least as much by intangibles as by the metrics we've been talking about. It is important to continually assess your current processes and overall approach to how you practice your security responsibilities and how that practice is perceived in your environment.

Here are a few questions to consider when making that assessment:

- Do my counterparts in the business see me as a true partner?
- Am I being called in at the beginning of new projects to help identify risks and develop mitigation plans from the outset?
- When changes in business processes and business models are being considered, am I involved?
- Do the metrics and reports I send out truly align with security risks and my strategic partners' concerns?

Success is not just a question of how well your organization is performing. It is also about how much personal and professional satisfaction you are taking in your role as a security practitioner.

So you should be asking yourself some serious questions about how you feel about your job:

- Do I truly feel valued by my superiors, my security colleagues, and my peers in the business?
- Does the company offer me the career path I am looking for, and am I doing everything I can to advance along that path?
- Am I doing everything I can to communicate the importance of what I do?

### 2.6.1.3 Your Answers Create Your Definition of "Success"

There is an important reason we based our definition of success on questions – and your individual answers to those questions. As much as you might like a straightforward way of defining your goals and determining whether you have achieved them, it's not that simple. It is a little like a child asking a parent, "When will I be a grownup?" It is easy to reply, "When you are eighteen years old" or "When you are at least five feet eleven inches tall." But, as is so often the case, the easy answer is not necessarily the right one. As we all know, lots of grownups are not five feet eleven, and lots of people over eighteen are not really grownups.

Your ESRM program won't be perfect from day one. (In fact, it will never be perfect, and recognizing that fact is a key component of a security practitioner's professional and personal maturity.) And it won't be measured by security or risk metrics, at least not in the meaningful way that ESRM requires. How will you know when you are successful? In some ways, it's similar to the difficulty of defining how mature you are. How mature is your organization? How mature are you at your security craft? How mature do you need to be or want to be, in order to accomplish your personal and professional goals? Of course, even when you feel like you have matured – either you individually or your entire program – it always feels like there is room for improvement.

ESRM is, in fact, a process of continuous improvement. As your security program becomes more successful, your strategic partners will rely on you more, and you'll know you are doing what needs to be done. And that is part of what success looks like: always recognizing that there is more to be done.

A good benchmark question for a security professional would be:

**Is our security program or my individual practice more mature today than it was yesterday?**

The answer won't be based on how many viruses you have blocked or how many dollars you have saved with your guard contract. It will be far more meaningful than that.

# Part 2

# Implementing an ESRM Program

**This part will help you to:**

- ➢ Prepare your security organization to adopt an ESRM methodology.
- ➢ Follow the ESRM life cycle steps to more effective security management.
- ➢ Design and roll out a new ESRM-based security program in your enterprise.

**3**

# Preparing to Implement an ESRM Program

Prior to implementing an ESRM program in your enterprise, there are some preliminary steps that you'll need to take to position yourself and your group to successfully start the ESRM cycle. In this section, we'll cover how you can prepare yourself and your program to follow an ESRM model. We'll also discuss the people outside of your security organization whom you'll need to involve in order to make the program a success in your enterprise.

## 3.1 Begin by Working to Understand the Business and Its Mission

The first step in the ESRM process is understanding. (That's a word you'll see us come back to over and over again.) It's impossible to understand the security measures you need to take to evaluate, mitigate, and protect against enterprise risks unless you understand what those risks are. And you can't understand those risks unless you understand the business – what it does and, crucially, why it does it.

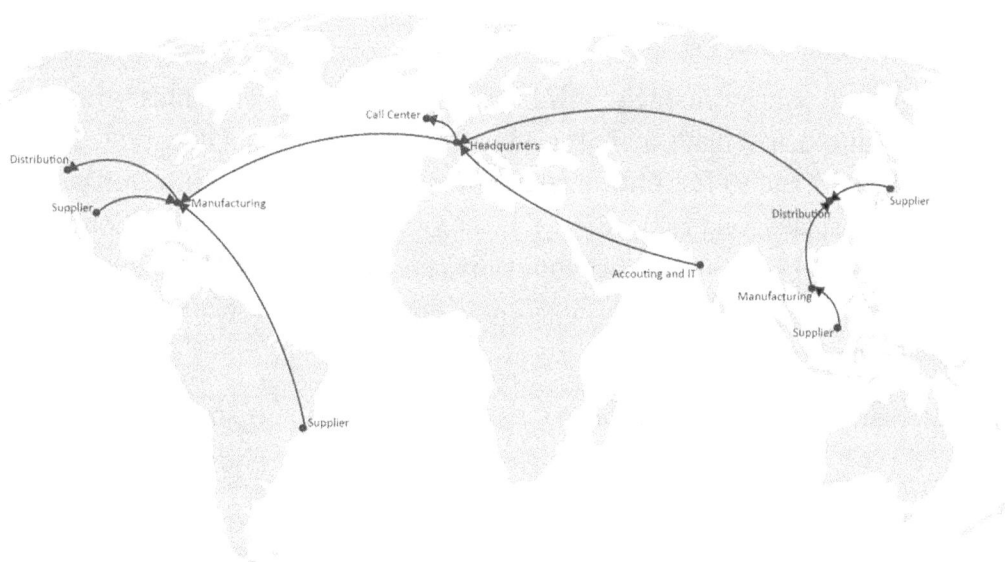

*Figure 3-1. Complexity in Enterprise Operations*

As you can see from the map in Figure 3-1, understanding your business is likely to be a complicated undertaking that involves many complex and interconnected parts, but it's absolutely necessary for implementing a successful security program.

An analysis by the leading consulting firm PricewaterhouseCoopers explains in detail why risk management activities (like ESRM) need to take into account the overall business context:

> It is important to begin by understanding the relevant business objectives in scope for the risk assessment. These will provide a basis for subsequently identifying potential risks that could affect the achievement of objectives, and ensure the resulting risk assessment and management plan is relevant to the critical objectives of the organization.

> Objectives are typically laid out in annual reports, business unit strategic plans, presentations to analysts, functional unit charters, project/investment plans, and management documents.... The focus on business objectives helps ensure relevance and facilitates the integration of risk assessments across the organization. (PricewaterhouseCoopers, 2008, p. 21)

Let's put that message in even plainer language: If you don't understand the business, its priorities and its objectives, you really can't even *begin* a worthwhile security risk assessment. Not only that, if you don't understand the role the security organization, and every security practitioner working in it, plays in the business, you can't protect the business.

Even if you've been working at a company for a very long time – maybe especially if you've been working there for a very long time – it's important to take a long, hard look at how the business is functioning now. (Security practitioners coming into an enterprise for the first time may actually have an advantage here, because they likely have fewer preconceptions about the way things work.)

Enterprises' missions change, as new products, new lines of business, and even entirely new business models are introduced, and that's more true now than it's ever been. Older products and services become less valuable, and so less critical as business risks, while new ones emerge. Industry drivers change constantly, and competitive threats and opportunities change along with them. All these factors need to be taken into account in any comprehensive, realistic security risk assessment, and the security practitioner's understanding of the business must be continuously updated, revised, and refined.

Here's an important lesson we've learned through years of managing security organizations and speaking with countless security practitioners:

> ➢ If your security program isn't clearly and realistically aligned with the needs of the business, it will be seen as out of touch at best, and a liability at worst.

This, in our view, is the primary source of the view of security as a stumbling block, as a function to be appeased, or worked around, or simply avoided, so that the business can get on with the business of running the business. And, as we've said – and will keep saying – that means you, as a security professional, have a mission-critical need to develop a deeper and broader understanding of the business environment.

There are many excellent references that can help you do that, including the International Organization for Standardization (ISO) 31000 Risk Management standard (2009) and the Committee of Sponsoring Organizations (COSO) Enterprise Risk Management Integrated Framework (2004) that we referenced earlier, as well as the American National Standards Institute/ASIS International/Risk Management Society (ANSI/ASIS/RIMS) Risk Assessment standard published in 2015. But the key lesson here is that your strategic partners and their needs should always be the key drivers in determining what matters to the business, and therefore to your success in protecting the business. That means you need to educate yourself about what the business needs and wants, and that education needs to be a continuous, iterative, ongoing process.

There are many ways to approach this process, but we believe there are three basic ways to understand the business and the associated risk environment:

- Listening to insiders.
- Examining the enterprise's internal and external messaging.
- Listening to outsiders.

Let's take a closer look at what this means in practice, by considering some of the questions we need to be asking ourselves and others.

### 3.1.1 What Are the Insiders Saying?

The simplest, most straightforward way to truly understand what is critical to the business is to talk – and, more importantly, listen – to the people who are running it on a day-to-day basis. They know how the business works; they know what's important; they know what assets represent the greatest business risks and business opportunities. As you work to understand their needs, the place to start is at the top, or as close to the top as possible. As we've already established, you can't have a successful security program without executive buy-in, so hearing what key executives have to say about the business's mission and objectives is essential. And what they have to say will help you understand other strategic partners' priorities, as well, and how they fit in the overall work of the enterprise.

Once you've heard what the executives have to say, talk to the people who run the enterprise's various lines of business. (We think you'll find that, like most people, they're happy to talk about what they do and why it matters.) Here are a few sample questions you can ask them:

- What product or service does your organization deliver, and what role does it play in the business's overall mission and goals?
- What is your organization's most important contribution to the business?
- How does your product or service work, and what resources – for example, skills, physical assets, or intellectual property – does your organization need to make it work?

- What are your organization's most urgent priorities, and what environmental factors can you see as potentially changing those priorities?
- What other internal organizations or outside resources do you rely on to meet your goals, and how well are those relationships working?
- What are the core values your team needs to be successful?
- What security risks are you most concerned about right now?

In many cases, these internal strategic partners are already aware of many of the risks they face and can lay them out for you very clearly. In others, your discussions will be a starting point for educating you about the business and educating your partners about risks. These conversations can be high-level, and in most cases they probably should be. They just need to be detailed enough to give you a nuts-and-bolts understanding of the business organization and how it works. And they'll have the added benefit of letting your partners know that you're genuinely interested in the needs of the business.

This process of getting to know your internal strategic business partners and what they need is a critical building block of the relationships – what we're calling strategic partnerships – that ESRM both creates and depends on to help drive success in the security program.

Getting people to discuss what they do, why they do it, and why it matters to the company is probably the simplest and most direct way to learn about the business and understand it. But it's not the only one. Let's look at some others.

### 3.1.2 What is the Business Saying About Itself?

Enterprises today spend an enormous amount of time, effort, and money communicating with the outside world: with their customers and clients, with their partners and vendors, with regulatory agencies and other government bodies, and, if they're publicly traded, with shareholders and industry analysts. All the information your corporate communications and public relations teams produces – from press releases to annual reports, from marketing collateral to regulatory filings – is important to the business. And it's all an excellent source of information that can help you, as a security practitioner, understand what's important to the business. Even a private company usually wants and needs to tell its story, and will almost always have an "About Us" page on its website that discusses its mission. Every one of these sources of information, though intended for others, can also be valuable to you as a security practitioner working to understand the business environment.

Many enterprises also have internal communications organizations that work to provide information to employees about different aspects of the company. The information they produce – on intranet sites, in training materials, and in policy manuals – can be an invaluable resource for the security practitioner.

Use all of these external and internal communications resources to gain a better understanding of these aspects of the enterprise:

- Vision, mission, and business goals.
- Values (often expressed in a mission statement).
- Organizational structure.
- Business plans and budget projections.
- Past risk assessments.
- Financial performance.
- Policies and procedures.
- Regulatory environment.
- Historical security environment.

Here's another extremely important source of information for security practitioners with publicly traded companies: the information that companies are required to make public by regulatory bodies like the US Securities and Exchange Commission (SEC). Your company's quarterly 10-K filing may make for heavy reading – and interpreting a 10-K probably wasn't part of your training – but there's no better source for information about your company's priorities and objectives. And you won't be relying on opinions or guesswork, because your company will have put a tremendous amount of time and effort into making certain that 10-K is absolutely accurate.

### 3.1.3 What Are Outsiders Saying?

A third way to understand the business is to see what other people – customers and clients especially, but industry analysts and the general public, as well – are saying about it. An online search will reveal many different perspectives on the enterprise, some of which you're likely to find surprising, and surprisingly meaningful. Here are just a few of the place you can begin looking:

- Mainstream news sources, like newspapers and online news sites.
- Specialized industry publications focusing on your enterprise's target markets (or adjacent markets).
- The financial media.
- Consumer and lifestyle publications and websites that feature both professional and nonprofessional product and service reviews.
- Competitors' advertising, especially if it offers different product or service comparisons.
- Online user communities.
- Social networks, like Facebook and Twitter.

Today's highly connected media world also offers you plenty of ways to learn about the world without even having to go out and look for information. Social media sites and news aggregators, like Apple News and Google News, can be set up to "push" information about subjects of interest directly to you. Say you want to keep in touch with political developments, travel advisories, or even weather reports from a location where your enterprise has a facility. Just enter a few keywords into a search engine, and you can have up-to-the-minute information in your inbox.

The relevant sources of information, and the types of information available, will of course vary depending on the enterprise and the industry. But one thing that won't vary is your need to seek out external points of view that can broaden and deepen your understanding of the business you're in and how it's being perceived in the real world.

### 3.1.4 What Isn't Being Said?

We don't mean to give you the idea that fully and deeply understanding your business will necessarily be easy. It isn't.

For example, any enterprise, any organization, has its own very specific culture, and the "rules" of that culture aren't always, or even usually, written down anywhere. There tends to be an assumption that "everybody knows" how things work – the assumption is frequently wrong, by the way – and for that reason, there's usually no formal documentation of the enterprise culture. But that doesn't make it any less important for you to understand.

The business writer and lecturer David Needle (2010) explains that what is usually called *corporate* or *organizational culture* is profoundly important, because it lies at the heart of literally every strategic or tactical decision or initiative the enterprise undertakes. It represents the collective vision, values, beliefs, and history of the enterprise. It's wrapped up in multiple factors, like product, market, location, and management style and is built on innate assumptions and attitudes that are picked up from all those factors.

So what are some of these unspoken assumptions that you should be looking for as you work toward a deeper understanding of the enterprise? Here are a few questions you could ask:

- Is this a suit-and-tie enterprise, or more of a flip-flops-and-foosball outfit?
  - o This may seem like a frivolous question. It's anything but. A highly regimented, disciplined enterprise will likely be receptive to a rigorous set of policies and procedures to mitigate security risk. A more casual, freeform environment may take more persuasion when it comes to accepting security measures – a lot more. (Interestingly, the two companies' risk tolerances might be essentially the same – the flip-flops-and-foosball outfit might have some extremely valuable intellectual property it can't afford to have leaked – but the security practices might have to be very different.)
- Is the enterprise historically resistant to change, or does it willingly embrace new ideas and ways of thinking?
  - o This is important because security changes are like any other type of change – new and uncomfortable and sometimes threatening – and you need to understand how open to change your strategic partners really are.
- How much risk is the company willing to take when it comes to certain vulnerabilities?

- The acceptance of residual risk – a concept we'll be returning to again later in this book – is central to the ESRM philosophy. And understanding how risk-averse or risk-tolerant the enterprise and its decision-makers are is central to the effective application of ESRM principles.
- How comfortable are key decision-makers with transparency as an essential security practice?
  - The need for business privacy is deeply ingrained in most senior executives, and that's especially true in certain industries that depend heavily on intellectual property, like high tech. Some business leaders may be worried about flaws in their processes and procedures being exposed. Understanding all these concerns will help you understand what your ESRM program can achieve, and what it may not be able to achieve.
- Will some business units and other internal organizations be more responsive to the idea of working with the security organization than others?
  - If so, why? This one is especially important, because it will give you a clear-eyed view of where you can begin your ESRM efforts, and where you can most effectively prioritize your efforts.

It's very important that you understand that what we're calling corporate culture isn't necessarily uniform or consistent. The unspoken, undocumented attributes that we're talking about can vary widely across the enterprise and even within internal organizations, and the larger and more complex the enterprise is, the more likely this is to be the case.

One of the best examples of how corporate culture can vary is high-tech. Software providers, especially startups, make a point of offering free and open environments as a way of attracting and retaining the talent they need – talent for which they're often competing intensely. So the work environments for some of their internal organizations, like programming, engineering, and marketing, are likely to be extremely relaxed. But what about the core of the business: the code, the core data, and the critical data centers that store and manage them. They're almost certainly going to have a much more "locked down" security environment. No unidentified employees wandering in and out there. And part of your role as a security practitioner will be recognizing, and accommodating, the difference.

That matters because you can't expect to force a security culture onto the business. A security organization operating on ESRM principles always – always – adapts the security culture to the business culture. ESRM isn't about creating and enforcing rules for the business to follow, an approach that almost invariably causes conflicts with the business it's trying to secure. Adapting security and risk approaches to the identified needs of the business both enables the business to function as needed and brings security risk to an acceptable level. And cultural understanding is absolutely essential to reaching that point.

### 3.1.5 What Is the Environment the Enterprise Operates In?

Enterprise environments vary widely, and their required levels of security vary widely as a result. For example, compare the security environment on a university campus with that of a defense contractor's manufacturing plant. A university is explicitly intended to be open, to encourage social interaction and the free exchange of ideas. A defense plant is almost exactly the opposite: a closed environment where workers, materials, and intellectual property are closely monitored to protect again espionage (including industrial espionage), sabotage, industrial accidents, and other disruptions. Security professionals designing policies and practices for such widely varying environments can't do that effectively unless they understand those environments.

Here are just a few basic questions to ask about the environmental aspects of the enterprise you've been tasked with protecting?

- What kind of area is the building or campus located in?
  - Many universities for example – however open and welcoming they may try to be – are located in areas with high crime rates that need to be taken into account.
- Is there a significant amount of traffic – on foot or in vehicles – in and out of the environment?
  - In some environments, people will be permitted to move freely onsite and offsite, while in others, ID will have to be checked and possibly bags searched.
- How many authorized people need to be on the site each day?
  - Some enterprise environments, like shopping malls and some government offices, are de facto public spaces, and will be visited by thousands of people every day who don't have any sort of explicit authorization to be there. Security measures for these environments, though obviously still very important, will necessarily be much more relaxed than in truly private environments.
- How much "public access" is required for the business to operate? How sensitive and critical are the business processes and assets that are onsite?
  - A defense plant can afford to keep visitors waiting while their identities are checked, but a retail store cannot.
- What are the expectations of the employees and management?
  - Many employers today go to great lengths to accommodate the lifestyle choices of their employees, as a way of recruiting and retaining the best and the brightest. (This is especially true of high-tech startups and their young knowledge workers, who can often pick and choose in a highly competitive market for talent.) That makes finding security measures that are not unnecessarily intrusive especially important.
- Will there be significant numbers of special needs persons coming in and out?
  - Accessibility sometimes requires special entrances and special accommodations, like checkpoints that are wide enough for wheelchairs to pass through and guidance for people with visual or auditory impairments.

This environmental understanding will be constantly evolving, because environmental aspects and needs can change very significantly, especially after a dramatic event. Virginia Polytechnic Institute and State University (Virginia Tech), for example, understandably would have a different security environment following the April 16, 2007 mass shooting that cost 32 people their lives. And, of course, even elementary schools now routinely issue panic buttons to teachers and practice lockdown drills, especially following the murders of 26 students, teachers, and administrators at Sandy Hook Elementary School in Newtown, Connecticut, on December 14, 2012. Even places that have historically been dedicated to openness and freedom of expression, like universities and grade schools, must now balance those values against the need to protect the environment and the people and assets within it. That requires the ability to make realistic decisions about acceptable residual risk – and to adapt to changing conditions on literally a moment's notice.

Those decisions aren't always easy, and neither is understanding the environment in which they'll be made, but Table 3-1 shows an example of why it makes a difference.

**Table 3-1. Comparing an Amusement Park and a Children's Hospital**

| An Amusement Park | A Children's Hospital |
|---|---|
| A vast, sprawling space that can function only with high, mostly unrestricted traffic flow through open spaces. Visitors don't want to feel that they're constantly being watched or followed, or to have their access to the places they want to visit restricted.<br>That isn't the experience people are looking for when they take their families to Walt Disney World or Six Flags, and isn't an experience that would be good for an amusement park's business. | A far less open space, with far more barriers to entry, both external and internal. Many of the areas in the hospital will be restricted to cardholders or other authorized personnel, and many will be openly monitored by uniformed security personnel and video cameras.<br>Most visitors won't be bothered in the least by these security measures. In fact, they'll likely expect to have to show ID before being allowed to visit a child's room, and they may well feel comforted by the presence of visible signs that their children are being protected. |

Here are two environments with some striking similarities: They're both designed to accommodate children and their parents, they're both high-volume, high-traffic, and high-density. And they both have a profound interest – professional, operational, and ethical – in protecting children. And yet it's almost impossible to imagine two more diverse environments from a security and risk perspective.

The approaches to security and risk management couldn't be more different, but neither is right or wrong. They're simply different – and the difference is based entirely on an informed understanding of the differences in the two environments.

### 3.1.6 Who Are the Environmental Decision-Makers?

It's important that you work to develop a comprehensive, evolving understanding of the environment you're tasked with protecting. But as part of the process – understanding the business, its changing priorities, and its risk posture – you also need to be aware of who is making the decisions about the business environment and the overall culture.

Remember, in an ESRM environment, your role isn't to make the business-critical security and risk decisions. It's to educate, provide guidance, and adapt the security culture to the business environment – not the other way around – and you can't possibly do that without knowing who the major players are. You'll need to be able to answer questions for your environment like:

- Who owns the business environment and the assets in it (for example, the operational head of a line of business, or possibly someone you're not even aware of yet)?
- Is the CEO responsible for the overall direction of the environment, or is the responsibility lower down on the management chain?
- Is the HR organization actively involved in guiding business-environment decisions to help recruit and retain employees?
- Are the employees themselves active in determining the type of environment they want to work in?
- Are legal or safety considerations critical to any aspect of the environment, due to laws or regulations like the US Occupational Safety and Health Act (OSHA)?

You'll need to answer all these questions – and many others – if you're truly going to understand the business you're charged with protecting.

## 3.2 Understanding Your Stakeholders – and Why They Matter

So now you've taken the important preparatory step of doing everything you can to understand the business, its products and services, its environment, its processes, its objectives, and its overall mission. Once you have a solid grasp of these fundamentals, you'll be in a much better position to set up a successful security program, because you'll know what needs to be secured and exactly what it is you need to protect – and, more importantly, why.

Now that you've developed an understanding of the "what" of the business, it's time to work on the "who." That means asking questions like:

- Who "owns" the business, or a specific segment of it?
- Who "runs" it?
- Who controls the assets that need to be protected?
- Who makes the final decisions about those assets?

These are critical questions, because they'll help you identify the people who are the key stakeholders in the process of protecting the business.

### 3.2.1 What Is a Stakeholder?

*Stakeholder* is a word we're going to be using throughout this book – it's a central ESRM concept – so let's start by defining exactly what we mean by the term. Here's an excellent business-oriented definition:

> Stakeholders are individuals or groups who have an interest or some aspect of rights or ownership in the project, can contribute in the form of knowledge or support, or can impact or be impacted by, the project (Bourne, 2005).

A stakeholder is also a person who ultimately has primary responsibility for an asset involved in a project or business. That asset can be almost anything: money, data, brand reputation, even a relationship (for example, with a regulatory agency) that could be damaged if not managed appropriately. And it's important to note that a single asset can have many stakeholders, because many individuals and roles can have that "concern or interest" noted in the definition above.

Whoever owns a business asset will ultimately be a risk decision-maker, either individually or together with others – sometimes many others. These stakeholders and the assets they own are intricately intertwined, and you'll need to determine who the main business stakeholders in a given area. The reason it's so important to identify these people is that ESRM is built on the concept of transferring the responsibility for security and risk decisions to the people who are responsible for those assets. And you can't do that if you don't know who they are.

### 3.2.2 Why Should You Care About Stakeholders?

Why does living an ESRM philosophy require identifying your stakeholders? What is the advantage to understanding your stakeholders before beginning to build out an enterprise security program or any individual security project? The answer, one that we'll be returning to again and again, is that these are the people who must accept the risk to the business of implementing – or not implementing – any security recommendations you make.

If you identify your most influential stakeholders early on and get their input to shape the goals, posture, and architecture of your program or project, your relationship with the stakeholders will help to:

- Ensure their support and improve the quality of the program or project model.
- Ensure that goals align with the needs of major stakeholders – helpful for the project and overall program at budget time. Let's be realistic: You can't make your program a success without the necessary resources, and those stakeholders don't just own the assets you're trying to protect. They also, in many cases, hold the purse strings.
- Ensure that they fully understand the security program, its roles and responsibilities, and its overall benefits. And stakeholders who understand the program – and especially stakeholders who have already had input into it – are far more likely to support it and give it priority over other, competing business pressures.

- Encourage these stakeholders to increasingly seek you out as a trusted partner to assist in risk identification and risk mitigation planning, one of the most fundamental indicators of ESRM success.
- Discover points of conflict or competing objectives among your stakeholders early, and develop strategies for resolving problems that might arise from these competing objectives.

These aren't the only reasons, but they're definitely some of the most important ones. It is essential in any security project to identify the individuals and groups within the business who will contribute to or be impacted by the projects, identify those who have something to gain and something to lose from any implementation, and then develop a strategy for dealing with them (Bourne, 2008).

Stakeholders are essential decision-makers. Their level of risk acceptance is important to your ESRM program because ESRM is both art and science. It requires that you balance an extraordinary range of security and risk priorities, protecting the business against threats while still allowing it to function. To take an extreme example, the simplest, and possibly the most effective, way to protect a building is simply not to allow anyone into it or near it. But of course that's almost always out of the question, because it would completely choke off the business's ability to operate and meet its objectives.

For example, in a retail environment, the business accepts the risk of allowing unknown persons into the location. It's not up to you as a security practitioner to say that risk is or isn't worthwhile. That decision must be made by the retail heads and other stakeholders. Your role is to listen to them, then design and implement security measures that they believe address their risks without impinging too far on their mission of selling products to customers. These measures may be as simple as security cameras to record activity in some locations, or as stringent as glassed-in enclosures to protect employees who are handling large amounts of cash or other valuables. The key to ESRM success, here as in the other types of businesses we've discussed, is to balance the need for acceptable security risk protections against the needs of the business and the people who make it work. That balance and deciding the tipping point is the realm of stakeholder risk acceptance and a major part of the art and science of ESRM practice.

### 3.2.3 What Is the Role of the Stakeholders in ESRM?

The stakeholders play an absolutely central role in ESRM. It is the stakeholders who make the crucial decisions on questions of risk mitigation, risk appetite, and risk acceptance.

In more granular terms, the stakeholders' role is to understand the assets they own or have an interest in. You can help them in this effort by helping them to clarify the value of their assets. Additionally, you can provide them more understanding of the assets by bringing them information on the threats that their assets are vulnerable to, how those threats could impact their business objectives, and explaining the security aspects of managing the risk of harm to their assets. The stakeholders can, and should, use their understanding of the business assets and objectives to assist in the development of mitigation planning and implementation – the best path to making the most appropriate risk decision.

### 3.2.4 Finding Your Stakeholders: A Closer Look

The process of learning about and understanding the business is going to give you a very good start on identifying your key ESRM stakeholders – but it's only a start. Think of all the people or groups who will be impacted by the security program or specific project, who will have influence or power over the completion of your projects, who will have an interest in the success or failure of the program or projects. These stakeholders may have an extraordinary range of roles, including senior executives, individuals in project or client organization roles, and system developers. And they may – and likely will – include individuals outside the enterprise, such as alliance partners, suppliers, customers, government entities, and the general public.

Take a look at who is impacted by the enterprise security program or specific project, asking yourself questions like:

- Who stands to gain from this project and who might be worried about losing?
- Who controls the necessary resources and who has the ultimate authority for the risk decision? And are they different people or roles?
- Who has influence as opposed to authority?
- What is my relationship with the stakeholder? Am I in a position to influence this person? Is it a reporting relationship?
- How much will I need to rely on influence – as opposed to direct authority – in working with the stakeholder?

It's important to identify stakeholders who have a vested interested in the success of your program. But it's every bit as important to identity any who may see security practice in general, and your recommendations in particular, as an impediment to succeeding in their goals.

You probably noticed that we used the word *influence* several times just now. That's because the stakeholders who will mean the difference between success and failure for your ESRM initiatives won't always be the obvious ones. Certainly, senior executives will be important. But in many cases, so will be individuals whose importance – and influence – is not necessarily reflected in a high-level title. Every enterprise has people like these: They're well-respected, they participate in important committees and meetings, they know how the company works – and sometimes have knowledge that nobody else possesses and that has never been documented – and they're valued by their peers and their superiors. For all these reasons, even though they may not be in formal positions of power, they have the ear of those who are.

That's why, when you're working to identify stakeholders, you must be careful not to concentrate too heavily on the enterprise's organizational structure, titles, and lines of reporting. Informal stakeholders, and groups of stakeholders, may have just as much power as the formal ones, and will need to be taken into account.

Stakeholders are, as we explained in the definition above, the people who have primary responsibility for various business assets, or are the additional risk decision-makers associated with those assets. There may be times when you find that an asset doesn't have a clear owner. In the ESRM process it's essential to identify an asset owner, who is also a risk stakeholder, in order to have an appropriate person to decide on risk tolerance, acceptance, or mitigation options. If an asset has no identified stakeholders, you must keep up the search for the right person. At times, this may mean you must keep going up the organizational hierarchy ladder to identify the asset owner or stakeholder. It is not your role as a security practitioner to decide who an asset owner is. As with most of ESRM, your role is to work through the process to ensure each asset that needs protection has an asset owner identified, and that your discovery process for stakeholder identification is thorough.

Here are a couple of real-world examples of how this process may work.

### 3.2.5 Example 1: Customer Personal Data – Whose Asset Is It?

Customer data is a critical asset for almost every business organization in existence, but let's get specific, and consider an account-based service: your local phone company. It stores and manages – and must protect – an enormous amount of sensitive personal data about its customers, including names, addresses, calling records and metadata, billing information, credit information, and payment methods.

So it's clear that all this customer data is a critical business asset; so it's crucial to find the appropriate stakeholder or stakeholders to make the risk decisions associated with it. But who is that?

- Is it the CIO, because the data resides on the IT organization's servers?
- Is it the customer care department, because it owns the customer relationship?
- Is it sales, because sales mostly gathered the information in the first place?
- Is it the chief privacy officer, because his or her role is to ensure that the company is protected from privacy liability issues?

So what's the answer? All of the above (and probably quite a few more).

If there was, for example, a data breach, all of those people and organizations would be engaged, because they would all have a role to play in the response and mitigation. And if they have a role to play in a breach response, then they clearly should also have a role in the decisions about how to protect, mitigate, and accept the risks associated with the data asset.

If you keep exploring, you'll probably find that the list of risk owners grows as your understanding of the business depends. For example, at the phone company, would the public relations department be a stakeholder? If the data breach received media attention, it would certainly be required to develop a response. What about the government relations group? Phone companies are closely regulated, and in most jurisdictions they would be required to report a breach of certain types of phone information within a predetermined period. So these organizations and roles should definitely be involved in the risk decision-making process, or at the very least be given an opportunity to review the risk decisions that the other stakeholders make.

This is, of course, a far cry from the traditional approach of simply letting the IT security department decide what protections should be in place to protect sensitive data. Of course, at the end of the day, the same protections might be put into place no matter who makes the decision or how the decision is reached. But that doesn't mean the process was excessive or unnecessary. What it does mean is that the security team responsible for securing the data reached beyond its traditional process, to involve all impacted stakeholders. And that matters, even if they all simply agree to go with whatever IT recommends.

### 3.2.6 Example 2: Customer Personal Data – Who Decides

But what do you, as a security practitioner, do when the stakeholders can't all agree on the appropriate treatment of risks? Let's continue with our customer data scenario, but with a very different type of business: an online stock trading service. The company's chief privacy officer will definitely want to ensure that customer data is securely protected and accessed appropriately, by the right people, at the right time, for the right reasons. But the customer service department has a business-critical interest in ensuring that the customer has a pleasant user experience that is informative, timely, satisfying, and hassle-free.

A company like this definitely needs a secure validation process for customers accessing their personal account information. The chief privacy officer may want extensive controls to protect customer data from falling into the wrong hands, and may request that the validation process be extensive and have several steps (possibly involving two-factor authentication). The customer service department, on the other hand, may be more concerned about annoying the customer and therefore streamline customer interactions. Clearly, these two stakeholders have very different, possibly even opposing, interests.

What is your role as a security practitioner in this scenario? Well, it's certainly not to take sides, even though your professional inclination may be to agree with the chief privacy officer that the most important issue is a more secure environment. It's extremely important that you take into account not only traditional security considerations, but also – and critically – the objectives of the business as a whole. You must manage the security risk process using risk principles. You have properly identified the risk owners: the chief privacy officer and the leader of the customer service department. Now you need to work through the process of helping those stakeholders find the best, most balanced, most workable solution to all their issues.

Remember, while you'll be weighing in with suggestions and guidance, the risk decision remains with – must remain with – the stakeholders. Helping them find the balance between their differing needs is the essence of ESRM. In this scenario, you might suggest an enforced password strength level that would satisfy the chief privacy officer while still leaving the customer with only a single authentication to go through. Whatever the final decision, facilitating a conversation and reaching agreement is the best way to reach the goal. Even so, if no agreement can be found, you may find that you must escalate the decision to executive management for a final decision.

# 4

# Following the ESRM Life Cycle

Once you have completed your preparatory steps of understanding your business and stakeholders, you can move into following the steps of the ESRM life cycle to begin implementing your program. We'll speak later in this book about an implementation and rollout project, but for now, we'll discuss the basic steps of the ESRM model and how to follow them.

## 4.1 What is the ESRM Life Cycle?

The ESRM life cycle (see Figure 4-1) is a phased process with four steps, some of which have separate subcomponents:

1. **Identify and prioritize assets.**
2. **Identify and prioritize security risks** (associate risks to assets).
3. **Mitigate prioritized risks** (mitigation planning or risk acceptance).
4. **Improve and advance.**
   a. Incident response.
   b. Root cause assessment.
   c. Ongoing security risk assessment.

*Figure 4-1. The ESRM Life Cycle*

If some or all of the steps in the cycle look familiar, that is a good thing. It means you're already familiar with at least some of the concepts that make up ESRM, and may already be practicing some of them. If you manage network security and you're configuring firewalls, for example, you're already implementing a mitigation plan. The same is true if you manage a business continuity program and have plans in place to respond to certain identified risks. But if you're not taking into account the entire end-to-end life cycle, you're not practicing ESRM – as we discussed earlier, you're just performing a discrete security task or a set of tasks.

While doing one or two of these things in your program is good (and that's how we used to operate our security program as well), the benefits of ESRM, of moving from task-based to risk-based management of your security program, are really only fully realized when you implement the holistic life-cycle of the program as we have defined it here. If you implement a mitigation plan like putting a guard in place in a sensitive location, but never revisit the risk that caused you to make that decision, as time goes on, your mitigation task of having a guard on the location may cease to meet the requirements for that risk. What if the sensitivity of that location goes down and you no longer need a guard? What if it goes up and the guards you have in place no longer adequately meet the risk profile? That's just an example, but as we work further through the process, you'll see how the life cycle of ESRM and the ideas of continual assessment and improvement work to make your security program more and more successful as time goes on.

## ESRM Life Cycle Defined

You're going to be seeing this term used throughout this book – it's absolutely central to the ESRM concept – so let's take a moment to clarify exactly what we mean by *life cycle*. Everything enterprises and organizations do, whether it's security-related or not, passes through a series of stages, from beginning to end. Now, the stages may be different, and they may change as the requirements and circumstances evolve, but we're still talking about a cycle. It's important to note that there isn't necessarily a starting point to the ESRM life cycle. It may be appropriate to jump into it at one step, but then shift focus to another step when a new risk emerges. However, all the stages in the life cycle are important, and they must all be understood clearly. And all of those stages – the end-to-end process of whatever it is you're trying to do – is the life cycle.

Every enterprise is different, with different security and risk requirements, and that means there will always be variations in the design and implementation of the ESRM life cycle, and especially in the level of detail involved. But there are some things every application of the ESRM life cycle will have in common, and one of the most important is that it will be a step-by-step process, with every step having a critical influence on all the steps that follow it. (At any particular moment in time, not every stage in the life cycle is as important as the others, of course, but every stage must be recognized and addressed, even if not all of them require significant action on the part of the security practitioner.) If you keep this basic principle in mind – if you always think in terms of moving through the steps of the life cycle in order – it will become an ingrained habit that you can apply to every security and risk issue you deal with, however large, however small.

We'll be referring again and again to the beginning and end of the ESRM life cycle, but it's important to understand that you won't always begin with Step 1. For example, you or your organization may already have completed Step 1 (Identifying and Prioritizing Assets), possibly without even thinking about it in those terms. And sometimes you'll find that after you have completed Step 2 (Identifying and Prioritizing Risk), a new risk has materialized or been identified, perhaps because of an unforeseen event, perhaps just because someone read something concerning in the newspaper. Or, crucially, a new risk may be identified simply because of the ongoing activities in the ESRM program – for example, as an unexpected result of an investigation into an unrelated event. When any of these things happen, it's important to go back to Step 1 – to understand how this new risk could affect business assets and objectives – before moving on to Step 3 (Mitigating Prioritized Risks). Keep this in mind as we walk through the ESRM life cycle of security risk assessments, and recognize that it is – and must be – a continuous thought process.

The ESRM model is a distillation of what we and other industry experts have been working with – proven approaches that we've seen work over many years in the security industry. In Table 4-1 we list several other widely used security models. You'll see similarities between all these models in the ways they approach identifying assets and risks, setting priorities, creating and implementing mitigation plans, and responding to security incidents.

These other models are all very useful and offer the security practitioner great insight, and we hope you'll refer to them as you enhance and refine your understanding of security and risk principles. But the ESRM model is different, with different focuses, different applications, and different goals. ESRM represents a comprehensive process of engaging asset owners and other stakeholders in the process of making risk decisions; partnering with other business function leaders to make security work as an integral component of the business; and working to be viewed not simply as an enforcer of arbitrary and unwelcome rules, but as a valued and trusted strategic partner.

**Table 4-1. Other Widely Used Security and Risk Models**

| | |
|---|---|
| European Union Agency for Network and Information Security (ENISA) Risk Management/Risk Assessment (RM/RA) framework | https://www.enisa.europa.eu |
| International Organization for Standardization (ISO) Enterprise Risk Management model | http://www.iso.org/iso/home/standards/iso31000.htm |
| National Institute of Standards and Technology (NIST) Cybersecurity Framework | http://www.nist.gov/cyberframework/ |
| ISACA Control Objectives for Information and Related Technology (COBIT 5) framework | http://www.isaca.org/cobit/pages/default.aspx |

Now let's take a closer look at the four steps in the ESRM life cycle.

## 4.2 Step 1: Identify and Prioritize Assets

The first step in the ESRM cycle, as shown in Figure 4-2, is understanding the enterprise assets – both tangible and intangible – that need to be secured as part of a security program or project, and, importantly, why they need to be secured. This will help you as a security practitioner to thoroughly address all of the security issues you've been entrusted with. And it will contribute to the overall success of your program, by positioning you to understand the business and what the business considers valuable.

*Figure 4-2. The ESRM Life Cycle –*
*Step 1: Identify and Prioritize Assets*

It may seem obvious, but this is absolutely critical: You don't want to use your time, effort, and resources to protect something that has little or no value. Even more important, you do want to protect things that have significant value – and you can't know how to do that it you aren't aware of their real-world value to the business. The ESRM approach, based firmly in the concept of understanding and managing risks to assets, positions you to see the whole picture, know where all the pieces of the picture are and, above all, how they relate to one another.

It's important to note that some assets – a factory, and the machinery and product inventory it contains – are obvious. But some assets are not so immediately recognizable. Take a service a third party provides to your company's customers, like technical support. It probably means the third party has at least some access to your company's data, which makes the service itself an asset that needs to be considered.

Earlier, you learned how to identify and approach your business stakeholders. Once you've done that, you can begin working with them to identify the assets that will be part of the program. This will happen at both the macro and micro levels: the macro level when a security program is being designed and implemented for the enterprise, and at the micro level for individual projects.

### 4.2.1 How Do You Identify Business Assets?

Identifying business assets – like identifying stakeholders – comes down to the kind of investigating we are all accustomed to as part of our security practice. Keep looking until you find everything there is to find. Identifying business assets is essentially the same. You just have to dig – and keep digging – because the enterprise's business assets will keep changing. Some enterprise assets will be easy to find, especially tangible assets like buildings, machinery, and product inventory. But you also need to consider more "conceptual" business assets, intangibles like brand reputation, goodwill (how people feel about your company), and industry relationships. Some assets can be both tangible and intangible, and some can have multiple owners – and a successful ESRM program must identify and consider them all.

That last part is extremely important. It's your responsibility as a security practitioner to seek out and identify business-critical, risk-critical assets. Traditional security practitioners sometimes wait for the business to come to them – or, worse, for a security problem to emerge – instead of making it their mission to uncover assets and the risks associated with them. The reality is, you aren't going to have the comprehensive understanding of the risks you need to address until you have the same understanding of the assets you need to protect. And nobody else is going to do the job for you.

## 4.2.2 Who Really "Owns" an Asset?

Once you've identified stakeholders and assets, you can get down to determining who the "owner" of any given asset really is. When ESRM principles are applied, as you can see in Figure 4-3, the owner of an asset is the person or organization with the greatest responsibility for the asset – the most "skin in the game," in sports terms. And figuring out who that is isn't always easy. Here are a couple of seemingly simple examples that show how complicated it can really be.

**A building.** Seems easy enough to identify the owner of this asset, doesn't it? It's a physical asset, and the facilities organization mostly takes care of maintenance, upkeep, that sort of thing, so facilities should be the asset owner, right? But now think about what goes on in the building: the people, processes, and business functions that are housed there. If it's a manufacturing plant or a warehouse, then procurement management may be the primary owner

*Figure 4-3. Multiple Asset Owners Can Share Asset Responsibility*

of the asset, because of the building's place in the company's supply chain. But if it's a call center, the customer service organization may have the biggest stake. If the building houses a data center, IT and information security have to be considered. And if the building contains multiple internal organizations – as the example shown in Figure 4-3 does – there are almost certain to be multiple asset owners including HR in any building that houses employees, and ultimately (mostly as an escalation point in any risk decision conflict) senior executives, as the ultimate layer of responsibility for the entire company.

**A server.** This example, at first glance, seems even simpler. A server is at the base level simply a computing device, so its owner should be someone in the IT organization who's responsible for keeping it up and running. But all that changes when you start to think about the applications that may be running on the server, or the processes that depend on it, or – crucially – the information that passes through it. Does the server hold payroll software? Then the accounting department obviously has a stake, and so does HR. Is it running computer-aided design (CAD) software?

Then the design, engineering, and manufacturing organizations may all be owners. And if the server stores sensitive personal data, it's almost certain that the regulatory compliance organization is one of the asset owners, along with the legal organization and possibly the government relations organization.

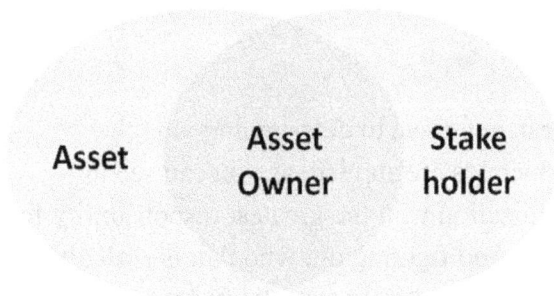

*Figure 4-4. Asset Owners Are Identified By Finding The Stakeholders With The Most Responsibility For That Asset.*

The point of this exercise – essentially, of finding the intersection of the stakeholders and the asset – is to identify the risk stakeholders. As seen in Figure 4-4, sometimes the asset owner and the risk stakeholder are the same person or the same organization. But that's not always the case.

## 4.2.3 How Do You Assign Value to Assets?

As we've already mentioned, you need to determine the value of the specific assets you've identified as a means of determining the appropriate security and risk measures to recommend to protect them. Some assets – especially tangible ones – are easier to value than others using common quantitative methods. We won't go into a lot of detail about this process here, partly because these methods are discussed in any basic accounting book and in online business finance resources like Investopedia.com and BusinessDictionary.com, and partly because this is a process that must be worked out with the business asset/risk owners and probably the finance organization, as well. But here's an overview of some widely used valuation methods.

## 4.2.3.1 Simple Tangible Asset Valuation (Two Methods)

There are two methods of simple tangible asset valuation:

1. **The cost method.** This method – probably the easiest to use – values an asset based on its purchase price. It's most useful when applied to stand-alone assets that have no complex dependencies on other assets (for example, in a supply chain).
2. **The market value method.** This approach values an asset based on its current market price, determined by one of two standards:
   - Replacement value – how much it would cost to replace the asset.
   - Net realizable value – how much the asset could be sold for.

Lost Orders
$100,000 Gear?

2 weeks offline
... $30,000 Gear?

$300 Gear

*Figure 4-5. Escalating Asset Value*

## 4.2.3.2 Complex Tangible Asset Valuation

Sometimes assets carry special dependencies – special circumstances that make valuing them more complicated and more difficult. Take a look at Figure 4-5 shown here as an example. A gear in a machine used on a manufacturing assembly line may have cost just $300 when purchased from a custom manufacturer. But if it fails, ordering a new one could take days, weeks, or even months, resulting in significant downtime and disruption, not to mention the work involved in replacing it and any other parts that might need to be replaced. And the manufacturer's customers may have service-level agreements (SLAs) written into their contracts that set financial penalties for failure to deliver products on time. Any one of these factors would make the gear's business value far higher than the $300 replacement cost, wouldn't it? That's why all associated costs and expenses must be taken into account. And getting that right depends heavily, if not entirely, on input from the business owner.

## 4.2.3.3 Intangible Asset Valuation

We've seen that valuing even tangible assets can be a very complex, difficult process – and the valuation of intangibles is far, far more difficult. The security practitioner will need to ask more questions, more probing ones, and involve many more people and roles.

To ensure the proper valuation of intangible assets – information, brand reputation, regulatory compliance, and other types – the security professional needs to involve a very broad range of stakeholders including (but not be limited to):

- Business leaders.
- The legal organization.
- The customer service organization.
- The corporate communications, public relations, and public affairs organizations.
- The corporate compliance organization.

## 4.2.3.4 Business Impact Analysis (BIA)

Another methodology for determining the value of assets – one that is used in many different risk-related programs – is the business impact analysis (BIA). In an ESRM program, a BIA focuses mainly on assets to determine how critical protecting an asset is, based on the impact the loss or compromise of that asset would have on the business's identified requirements, objectives, and needs.

Like our other asset valuation methods, the BIA process has entire books and websites dedicated to it. You may have teams in your company that perform disaster recovery or business continuity, or financial or other types of risk management, who can help you with the BIA process. The International Organization for Standardization (ISO) has standard ISO 22301 that goes into the BIA process in depth. Additionally, books such as *Enterprise Risk Assessment and Business Impact Analysis: Best Practices* by Andrew Hiles can provide valuable insight. As it's too big a topic to cover in this small space, we recommend you learn more about it from one of those valuable sources.

### 4.2.4 How Do You Prioritize Assets for Protection?

The outcome of the asset valuation process is a value that can be used to determine the priority or level of protection needed for each asset. It seems obvious that assets that have little or no real-world impact on the business should have less rigorous protections applied to them than high-impact assets. However, business asset owners often ask for protections that extend far beyond what we as security practitioners see as the true value or impact of a given asset. Dealing with that disconnect becomes much easier when you have the results of the impact analysis to back you up.

The priority of assets is, of course, ultimately up to the business owners – that's one of the most fundamental principles of ESRM, and one we can't lose sight of – but it's important for you as a security practitioner to give your stakeholders all the information they need to make the right decision and help the asset owner understand that information and its implications. That means making sure the business units are aware of the impact of a possible security failure, are aware of all the different opinions on the impact, are aware of your professional security-based opinion on what protecting that asset might include, and consider any future impact of the asset. Keep in mind, too, that when you work with the asset owner on valuing the assets in the first place, and help them identify, explore, and answer the questions of impact, value to the organization, and risk exposure, they are far less likely to have unrealistic expectations on priorities of their assets in the first place – limiting that disconnect we mentioned above.

### 4.2.5 How Do You Deal with Conflicts in Asset Valuation and Prioritization?

As we've seen, a specific enterprise asset can have multiple owners and stakeholders – and owners often disagree on the value of that asset. Here's one fairly typical example: Let's say you're a security practitioner with a company that does some of its sales online. The company's public-facing website is the online sales manager's top asset, and her annual performance bonus is 90%, based on site traffic and sales, and that makes it her top priority. She urgently wants the asset to be protected with significant data security and business continuity controls, including fully redundant servers, and continuous backup of databases. But the IT director thinks the existing failover backup solution is adequate, and doesn't want to incur the costs of the additional protections.

As a security practitioner, your role in the valuation process is to guide the business and the stakeholders through a conversation – a conversation that's informed by your analysis of asset value and associated risk – and help them find agreement on the appropriate level of risk the business is prepared to accept and the appropriate protections to put in place to address that level of risk.

Now back to our example: What if the asset valuation process shows that the website accounts for less than one percent of the company's total sales? What if online sales simply aren't a core part of the company's current strategy? How important is the website, and what is the appropriate cost of protection? Are the costs of the protections the online sales manager wants worth the potential benefits?

Nobody is saying that the company shouldn't take steps to mitigate security risks in this situation, or any other. But it's definitely important to prioritize resources in line with the overall business mission and with goals that have already been thoroughly investigated and are clearly understood by the asset owners and all other stakeholders.

This is a good time to stress again – as we will throughout this book – the importance of understanding the business and having great relationships with your strategic partners. You will definitely find times when there are conflicts among asset owners about how they value and prioritize their assets. And there will probably be times when you have to make the uncomfortable decision to escalate a conflict to senior business leaders for a definitive resolution. A clear, detailed, comprehensive understanding of the enterprise's mission, vision, and goals, as well as strong ongoing relationships with executives and senior leaders, can be of incalculable value in helping you guide the business through conflicts over asset valuation.

## 4.3 Step 2: Identify and Prioritize Risks

The next step in the ESRM life cycle, as seen in Figure 4-6, is to determine the risks that may impact the assets that have been identified and prioritized, and develop an associated risk profile. This makes it possible to create mitigation plans for minimizing the probability of those risks becoming realized or minimizing the potential impact if they are realized. Risks can vary in what sometimes seem to be an infinite number of ways, and understanding all the variables involved can be extremely challenging.

*Figure 4-6. The ESRM Life Cycle – Step 2: Identify and Prioritize Risks*

The process of identifying, associating, and prioritizing risk – a process that is most commonly known as risk assessment – is a common topic in many disciplines, not just ESRM. That's why this section includes some common definitions from the International Organization for Standardization (ISO) risk standard 31000.

### 4.3.1 How Do You Assess Risk?

The ISO (2009) defines a risk assessment as the overall process of risk identification, risk analysis, and risk evaluation. Let's take a closer look at the three components of that definition.

- Risk identification is finding, recognizing, and detailing the risks that could impact the asset under consideration or the business mission objectives the asset is tied to.
- Risk analysis is understanding the nature, causes, and origination points of the identified risks and estimating the level of risk. Analysis also includes determining the potential impact of the risk to the business whether financially or through operational impacts, or even intangible impacts, such as reputational effect, and identifying any existing controls that the business might already have in place for the risk.
- Risk evaluation compares the results of the analysis with the overall company risk tolerance level and management acceptance criteria in order to determine if a risk is tolerable or must have mitigation steps identified.

In the next few sections we'll break down how you perform these three steps to come to a plan for allowing business owners to understand and either accept or mitigate the discovered risks.

### 4.3.2 How Do You Find All the Risks?

In Table 4-2 we outline a number of possible risks to look for. Some risk assessment is simple and straightforward. "Hard" assets, like buildings, are exposed to a readily identifiable set of environmental risks based on their location. An enormous amount of readily available data – information on flooding and weather history and seismic fault lines – can help you determine many risks. Crime statistics can help to determine what risks may be present in a specific area, too. And, of course, some risks are obvious simply because of the nature of the enterprise's business. A defense contractor that handles classified government data – or the Internal Revenue Service (IRS), with its huge stores of sensitive information about hundreds of millions of individuals – must be deeply concerned with information security, while a gold mine is likely far more concerned with the risk of theft. The risks listed in Table 4-2 are clearly not the only ones to think about, but they represent a good starting point for a discussion of security risks.

**Table 4-2. Risk Examples**

| Risk Category | Risk Types |
|---|---|
| Financial | - Asset protection/security<br>- Theft of product or service<br>- Fraud |
| Business continuity and resiliency | - Transportation, logistics of supply chain disruption<br>- Crisis events<br>- Product deployment security |
| Cyber | - Distributed denial-of-service (DDoS) attack |

| | |
|---|---|
| | • Cyber extortion<br>• Hacktivism |
| Reputation and ethics | • Customer data loss<br>• Corporate governance failure |
| Human resources | • Employee misconduct<br>• Labor disputes |
| Information | • Intellectual property theft<br>• Privacy infringement<br>• Network intrusion<br>• New technologies |
| Regulation and liability | • Regulatory compliance<br>• Audits<br>• Litigation |
| Physical | • Inventory loss<br>• Access control<br>• Political instability and social unrest |

Not all risks are as obvious as these, however. You also need to be aware of business-specific risks or other risks that might not be immediately apparent. A good place to start is to stop thinking like a security practitioner – if only for a little while – and approach risk assessment from the point of view of some other key stakeholders.

- **Think like a CEO.** The CEO's "big picture" concerns will center on security risks that could impact the company's ability to carry out its mission, cause it to lose customers or market share, and keep it from being profitable. Those risks will inevitably vary widely. In a retail environment, the highest priorities might be protecting customer information and preventing theft by customers or employees. In a research facility, the most important concern might be keeping trade secrets from walking out the door. In a heavily regulated business, such as a brokerage firm, there may be nothing more critical than meeting the Securities and Exchange Commission's regulatory compliance requirements. And in a critical infrastructure environment, like an energy utility, the highest priority may simply be keeping the lights on. Once you understand the CEO's key concerns, you'll have a better and more actionable understanding of the risks you need to address.
- **Think like a shareholder.** Most shareholders' first concern, of course, is the profitability of the company they've invested in. But even that seemingly simple concept, and the risks associated with it, can be difficult to define. Take the 2013 Target data breach, for example. Target's shareholders definitely saw the value of the company's customer data after the breach in 2013 (Prince, 2015). In an analyst call in 2014, the company's CEO, Brian Cornell, estimated the total cost of the data breach at $191 million, for a net cost of

$162 million after insurance payments were taken into account. The financial impact to the company of not providing adequate security to customer data definitely meant a lot to the shareholders – and in fact the breach was a contributing factor in costing Cornell's predecessor as CEO his job. Could Target's security practitioners and assets owners have predicted a $162 million price tag for a data breach? Probably not. But thinking like shareholders would probably have helped them take the threat more seriously than they did.

- **Think like a customer.** This is a little easier, because we've all been customers, and we've all had good and bad customer experiences. So put yourself in the place of your organization's customers and imagine what their major concerns might be. Is it their personal safety when they're on your premises? Is it keeping their private information out of the hands of thieves? Is it ensuring that your services are always available? Let's say you're responsible for security for a telephone company. Now, you and the company probably have a specific view of the value of a single telephone call placed on a landline: probably something like what it costs the company to make that call possibly, compared with what the customer pays for it. But does the customer see its value the same way? Probably not. If it's a call to order a pizza, it's not necessarily a high-value asset for the customer. But if it's a call home on Mother's Day – or an urgent call for an ambulance in the middle of the night – its value is obviously very different. And if the customer doesn't have a mobile phone, and so lacks an alternative method of communication, the call becomes even more valuable.

These are all different ways of valuing an asset and, more importantly, different ways of looking at valuing an asset. And they don't necessarily contradict one another. The CEO, the shareholder, and the customer – and many other stakeholders – all have their own "right" ways of establishing the value of an asset. What matters, from an ESRM perspective, is considering all their viewpoints so that you, as a security practitioner, can conduct a thorough and meaningful risk assessment.

### 4.3.3 How Do You Prioritize Risk?

Once you've identified all your stakeholders, worked with them to value all the assets that need protecting, then developed a list of risks to those assets, it's time to prioritize the risks you've identified. Which risks are the most important, the ones that most urgently require mitigation plans? Which risks might be acceptable to the business?

This is the point at which all of the information you've gathered – about corporate culture, acceptable levels of risk, what's most important to the stakeholders, what exposures each asset has, and what the impact of the asset might be on the business – comes together, so that you can use it to start planning a security strategy for protecting the enterprise and its assets.

When you're prioritizing risk, you can go back to the concept of the risk triangle. As shown in Figure 4-7, the risk triangle states that in order for a risk to exist, it requires three things:

1. A threat.
2. Exposure.
3. Impact.

A threat is something that could potentially impact an asset. Threats could include an act of violence, theft, a cyber-attack, fraud, fire, flood, vandalism, an information

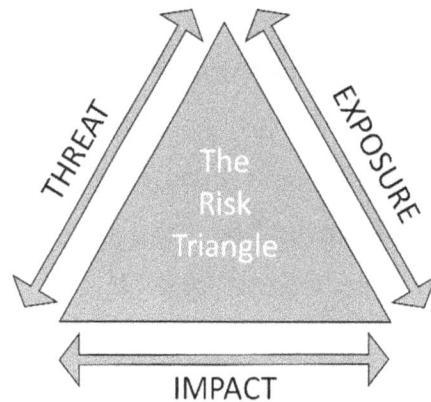

*Figure 4-7. The Risk Triangle*

security breach and/or almost any other security incident. However, a threat on its own doesn't pose a risk.

The threat of flood, for example, doesn't impact an asset that is far from any flood zone. This is because there is no second side of the triangle – exposure. Exposure is the level to which any particular threat might actually happen to the asset in question. A building far from a coastal area has very little hurricane risk due to a very low exposure rate, and an asset that is very heavy and extremely difficult to move has a low exposure to theft.

The final side of the risk triangle is impact. Impact of the risk to the business can be financial or operational, or even an intangible impact such as reputational effect. Impact considerations must also identify any existing controls that the business might already have in place to avoid the risk. To move back to the flood example, an asset may be near a river, and therefore exposed to the threat of flood, but if the asset is submersible, there is no impact to it and thus still no risk. Only when the three aspects come together does the risk materialize as an item to be considered in the assessment process.

The threat level, the exposure level, and the impact level all combine to determine what order of importance the risk should be considered in. In this step, your role as a security practitioner is to build a matrix of risks, and even to preliminarily prioritize them for mitigation. But it's important – in fact, it's absolutely critical – that business owners and other stakeholders must be engaged in discussions at this point, to determine how the business sees the risk and whether they are willing to accept the risk or wish to find a method for dealing with it.

New risks materialize every day. That's why situational awareness is incredibly important for any security practitioner. You need to be continuously learning about new threats and actively scanning for threats that could impact the company's assets. That's especially critical because risks change constantly, rapidly, and in many unforeseen and sometimes unforeseeable ways – and as a security practitioner, you need to be ready to recognize them and address them. If the new risk isn't a priority it can be dealt with through the typical security management program. If it's a new risk and is a priority, communication of the risk and mitigation plans may have to be expedited. The security landscape is always changing, and as practitioners it's what will keep you on your toes.

## A Risk Prioritization Case Study: The "Small" Fraud That Isn't Small at All

Risks will be different for different assets, but can even be different for the same asset, based on the perspective of the stakeholder looking at the risk and the surrounding circumstances.

Here's an example that shows how different risk priorities can be – and how they can change. Let's say you're working for a major lending institution. A mortgage broker is suspected of setting up fraudulent accounts, collecting sales commissions on the mortgages associated with those accounts, then letting them go into default for nonpayment.

*Figure 4-8. The ESRM Life Cycle – Step 3: Mitigate Prioritized Risks*

An investigation establishes that the broker did, in fact, commit the fraud, and he's immediately fired. Does that mean there is no longer any risk? Or is it still a priority? The other brokers, their managers, sales executives, company executives, and investigators all see this from their own unique, and very different, perspectives.

The salespeople probably just want to get back to work, so they're likely to see the firing of that one employee as all that was needed to mitigate the risk the fraud presented. They see the risk as a low priority. But is that their decision to make? Or, to put the question in ESRM terms, do they own the risk? If the investigation showed that only 1% of the company's sales were impacted by the fraud, the issue would probably stop there. The company's senior executives probably wouldn't think much about, and might not even want to be informed.

But what if further investigation showed that more than just that one employee were using that fraudulent process – and that the fraud actually represented something closer to 5% of total sales. Would that make the risk a higher priority, and warrant escalation of the issue to senior executives? What if the fraud was on such a large scale that it might force the company to restate its quarterly earnings? It no longer seems quite such a low-priority issue, does it?

And, of course, it could always get worse. (If there's one thing we know as security professionals, it's that things can always get worse.) What if the investigation showed that certain managers on the sales team had known about the fraud and covered it up so that the company wouldn't have to restate its earnings? Wouldn't everyone's perspective change at that point? Remember, senior corporate officers sign off on Sarbanes-Oxley forms saying that those earnings reports are accurate – and if they're not, they and the company are both liable for very serious civil and even criminal penalties.

Yes, this is a lot of "What if?" questions. But "What if?" is what risk identification and prioritization is all about.

## 4.4 Step 3: Mitigate Prioritized Risks

As you can see in Figure 4-8, the next part of the ESRM process centers on mitigating the risks that you've identified and prioritized.

The ISO risk management standard 31000:2009 discusses mitigation as part of a larger topic of *risk treatment*. The standard tells us that risk treatment is a "process to modify risk." The ISO goes on to modify that broad definition with a few clarifying notes.

- "NOTE 1 Risk treatment can involve:
  - avoiding the risk by deciding not to start or continue with the activity that gives rise to the risk;
  - taking or increasing risk in order to pursue an opportunity;
  - removing the risk source (2.16);
  - changing the likelihood (2.19);
  - changing the consequences (2.18);
  - sharing the risk with another party or parties (including contracts and risk financing); and
  - retaining the risk by informed decision.
- NOTE 2 Risk treatments that deal with negative consequences are sometimes referred to as risk mitigation, risk elimination, risk prevention and risk reduction.
- NOTE 3 Risk treatment can create new risks or modify existing risks." (International Organization for Standardization, 2009)

Keeping that definition in mind, let's explore the ESRM approach to that process. In our model, we refer to this step of the ESRM cycle as *mitigation* because that is the most typical response to risk. There are, however, a few other options, as we outline below.

### 4.4.1 Risk Treatment Options

As we've said already: The final decision on what to do to treat a particular business risk is up to the business owner of that risk. Still, it's important for the security practitioner to be able to provide options to assist the business owner in making that decision. Typically, there are four options for dealing with any risk.

1. **Accept the risk.** The business owners have ultimate responsibility for their own areas, and the risks associated with them. They may choose to accept a given risk, if they think that's appropriate.
2. **Stop the activity that causes the security risk.** This is always an option that should be considered. Is the activity that the business is engaging in worth the risk taken on by doing it? For example, is operating a retail store – one that handles a lot of cash and other valuables – in a high-crime area worth the risk? Perhaps the answer is yes. The outlet may be highly profitable, and there may be legal or regulatory obstacles to refusing to operate in an underserved area. For these reasons, the risk owner might decide to continue to operate the outlet, despite the risks to both property and employees. But the

risk owner might also decide that the risk is unacceptable, and mitigate it by simply ceasing operations.

3. **Transfer the risk to another party.** Simply put, this is typically a matter of purchasing insurance to pass off the financial impact of a risk to a third party, or having a partnering company indemnify your company against a risk. The impact might still occur, but if the asset in question is easily replaced and not time-critical, transferring the risk might be a good option.

4. **Mitigate the probability or impact of the security risk.** This is the area where your skills and knowledge as a security practitioner will likely prove to be most valuable. You can identify the threat, and determine what security measures could reduce the enterprise's vulnerability to the threat, the likelihood of it actually happening, and the impact if it does happen. This means developing business-case-based mitigation recommendations for the risk owners to consider. (**Note:** Because our response to risk is to mitigate the exposure or impact, a vast majority of the time, common usage tends to refer to all risk treatment as mitigation. In this book, we'll reference mitigating the risk, because that's where security has actual tasks to perform. However, it's crucial to remember that this is only one of the treatment options.)

Your role as a security practitioner is, again, to manage the process of dealing with risk, so the risk owner can decide on the appropriate risk mitigation plan. Of course, you're the security professional, and your recommendations and solutions are key to the process. But it's central to ESRM to provide the owner of the asset and risk with information to show them what options will have what level of protection. Some small steps might provide enough protection benefit that your risk owner might feel that is enough and not implement a larger project. If it's truly their risk to accept, and you've communicated the risk appropriately so that they truly understand what they are accepting, then implementing their chosen option is the correct path.

### 4.4.2 Who Has the Final Word on Risk Mitigation?

While your role as discussed above is to present risk mitigation options to the business and work with your stakeholders to determine the best risk mitigation choices, you, as the security professional, also need to be aware of which stakeholder has the ability to make that choice. If the risk response is being decided at the wrong level, or if it's being accepted by the wrong party, it's your role to point this out and either escalate it to the right party or bring in the proper (or additional) risk owners. This can be a tricky process, but it may be the most important part of ESRM and definitely takes the most interpersonal skill.

Why is it tricky? Because, inherently, escalating a risk or even bringing in additional risk owners may feel to the person who has identified themselves as the risk owner that their discretion and authority are being challenged. Even if all the right words are being used, the escalation of risk acceptance may be perceived as a challenge. Additionally, it can be difficult on the other side to bring in additional risk stakeholders because most people in the business think acceptance of a risk equals accountability should something go wrong.

Both sides of escalating risk acceptance or mitigation choices can be contentious, but that is the main role of the security department in the ESRM model and when done properly is the main benefit to both the business and the security group in knowing that security risks are being properly treated according to the risk acceptance tolerance defined by the business itself.

All these discussions require the business to look upon you in your security role as a trusted partner. While we've discussed some tactics already in this book on gaining the credibility to be that trusted partner, here are some additional tactics you can use to make sure the business knows that you are there to assist them in securing the business, not to "throw them under the bus."

## 4.5 Step 4: Improve and Advance

We talked in section 4.1 about ESRM being a cycle. The improve and advance step of the cycle shown in Figure 4-9 is where the flow gains the momentum needed to swing back around to the beginning. In order to make sure your program is successful, you must be continually scanning and reassessing your program, environment, responses, and business. ESRM is a continuous, ongoing process, involving:

1. Incident response.
2. Root cause analysis.
3. Ongoing risk assessment.

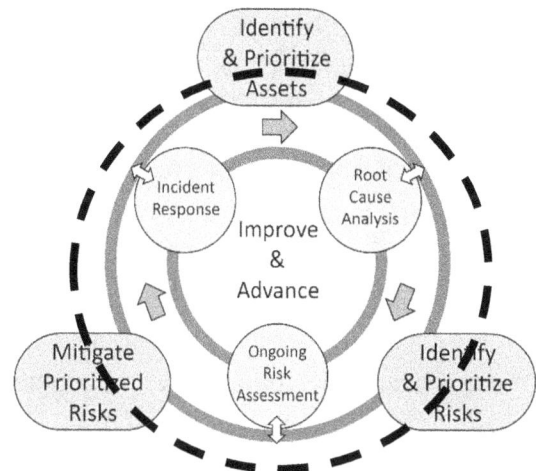

*Figure 4-9. The ESRM Life Cycle – Step 4: Improve and Advance*

These are the sub-steps that allow you to improve and continue to advance your ESRM program once it's in place.

### 4.5.1 Incident Response

Continually improving and advancing your ESRM program requires that you recognize the inevitability of security incidents occurring, and respond to them when they do. It is an important component of your role as a security practitioner to discover incidents or new risks that the security organization – and the larger enterprise – will need to handle in some way.

Incident response can mean one of two things:

- A reactive response – reacting to an incident of harm coming to the enterprise.
- A proactive response – reacting to the identification of potential harm that could occur due to some activity that is actively occurring.

In the first, an "event" will occur and need to be dealt with in some way. This could be anything from an angry customer in a retail environment who needs to be escorted off premises, to responding to a bank robbery (if your security team is trained and tasked with such things). The second type of incident response is where information is brought to the security department about behavior or activity that is not actively causing harm, but has the potential to do so if not dealt with. Examples of things that fall into this category are reports of concerning behavior that falls into the "red flags" zone of the workplace violence spectrum or perhaps a report of network activity that looks suspect but may or may not be an actual cyber-attack.

Both types of incidents are things the security team will react to and provide some kind of protective action for the enterprise.

Incident response is an ongoing response to security incidents that are specifically reported or brought to the attention of security by internal or external sources and is one way to maintain awareness of impacts to the enterprise from previously unknown or residual risk.

Once an incident has occurred, and the immediate response of life safety, damage control, and stoppage of immediate impact is complete, the next step in the continual improvement process is to perform an investigation into the incident to discover the root cause.

## 4.5.2 Root Cause Analysis

Investigations are a core part of all security programs, not only ESRM. As a security practitioner, even if you are not directly the investigator, you should still be aware of the general investigation process and how investigations into all types of security incidents can drive overall improvement of the security environment in your organization. In the ESRM model, although investigations for the sake of determining the perpetrator of an incident are, of course, a part of the security incident response, the main goal of all ESRM investigations is to discover the true root cause of the incident – to understand the risk that was behind it and determine whether residual risk still exists. Just as we discussed two types of incident response, there are two types of investigations that we consider:

- A **reactive investigation** is performed as part of the analysis of any incident response (of either the reactive or proactive type). These are investigations into the facts surrounding an incident impact such as determining who perpetrated a theft and what circumstances may have contributed to it occurring, or an investigation into reported suspicions – perhaps a tip from someone about possible sales fraud, or time card issues based on questionable form management.
- A **proactive investigation** is the process of scanning the environment for threats from inside or outside, such as new social engineering techniques, or intelligence-gathering on internal personnel who may be exploiting vulnerabilities of the business, looking at changing demographics in an area that might lead to new risk, or monitoring virus registries to understand emerging cyber threats.

Both types of investigation are, in the ESRM paradigm, driven by the goal of determining the security risk that was at the foundation of the incident or potential incident. This is what we refer to as *root cause analysis*.

Root cause analysis flows from and is part of the response and investigation process. Sometimes security practitioners feel that once a threat has been identified and neutralized, or incident impact has been stopped, their job is done. But that is not always – or even usually – the case. In ESRM, the root cause analysis, or "postmortem report," is a vital aspect of continually improving the program, and especially identifying and mitigating residual risks.

This root cause analysis is the critical activity that will enable you to improve and advance your program.

Postmortem analysis includes asking follow-up questions and delving into the answers to determine root cause, residual risk left from that cause, and actions that might prevent the incident from recurring.

- What happened?
- What were the time lines of the event?
- How did it happen?
- Could this happen again?
- What was the threat?
- Has the threat changed?
- What was the exposure?
- What was the attack path or vector?
- Were there any controls in place and if so what controls were circumvented or failed?
- Do the same vulnerabilities still exist that could be exploited again?
- Do changes need to be made to mitigate the probability and potential impact or is accepting the same risk acceptable again?

Once the postmortem report is complete, you should provide the report to the impacted business units and other stakeholders as part of your ongoing strategic partnership. The report will make your partners aware of any previously unknown or residual risks that were discovered in the investigation and allow them the opportunity to treat those risks, just as they had that opportunity in the first pass through the ESRM cycle.

### 4.5.3 Ongoing Security Risk Assessment

Incident response, investigations, and root cause analysis all feed directly into – and really are aspects of – the last piece of continual improvement, which is constantly assessing and updating the company picture of risk – because risk is continually evolving and changing – and because residual risk may be discovered during the ESRM process.

Ongoing risk reassessments are also good for the program overall, because if ESRM is a continual process, each iteration involves less time and effort than a full assessment "from scratch" would require.

When circling back around to perform a reassessment, some of the questions to ask yourself are:

- What's new in the environment?
  - What assets have been purchased?
  - Has the business reorganized into different business units?
  - Has the business launched any new products?
  - What new projects are in the beginning phases that the security group could provide input on from the start?
  - Have new regulations from external agencies been released?
  - Are there any new risks?
  - Have previously identified risks become more significant?
  - Are there new mitigation tools that would be more effective and efficient to minimize risk?
  - Have previously implemented mitigation plans and/or tools become outdated and no longer effective against an existing risk?
  - Are there any emerging risks that should be anticipated?
- What's been depreciated or retired since the last assessment?
  - Have any products been pulled from the market?
  - Are some services no longer being offered?
  - Have systems been replaced or retired completely?
  - Have policies or procedures been retired or changed?
- Have postmortem recommendations been followed or completed?
  - Has the mitigation process been completed for risks found through the last assessment?
  - If not, why are open issues still open?

The answers to these questions will point you in the direction of new stakeholders to talk to, or perhaps help you identify stakeholders who can be removed from the list. They will help you narrow down where to look for new assets or allow you to remove some assets from the assessment list. You can use these questions to drive discussions with business units to see if their goals and objectives have remained the same, and if their appetite for risk has been impacted by any of the changes.

A final thought: All of these processes, like all the other elements of ESRM, are targeted at helping the business – the risk owners – make the right decisions in the right way. But it's not your role, as a security professional, to "fix" the problem. Once you've made your recommendations, and given all the stakeholders involved the information and guidance they need to make an informed decision about either mitigating risk or accepting it, it stops being your responsibility and becomes part of the role of the asset owner and risk stakeholder to carry out a response as they deem appropriate.

# 5

# Phased Rollout

The key to putting ESRM into practice enterprise-wide will be learning to think, and communicate, more like your partners on the "business" side of things. In this section, we are going to introduce you to a widely used business concept called *design thinking* that product and process developers across many different industries and in many different organizations use to roll out products, services, and internal programs. Then we'll show you how to tailor the concepts of design thinking into a phased, iterative rollout plan for your ESRM program. This thought and program design process will make developing and releasing your ESRM program much easier as you learn to interact more effectively with your strategic partners in developing security programs that meet their needs as well as yours.

## 5.1 Design Thinking – A Conceptual Model for Your ESRM Program

There are plenty of worthwhile methodologies out there for conceptualizing business programs, processes, and products. (It's important to understand that we're not just talking about security programs here. These methodologies apply to all aspects of business.) One that we've found very useful is what has come to be known across business organizations as *design thinking*. Design thinking is now widely used in business as a way of helping decision-makers identify problems and issues and develop and implement creative yet focused solutions to them. (**Note:** We wish to acknowledge the work of David M. Kelley at Stanford University in developing the *design thinking* methodology we are using (Kelley & Kelley, 2012, December). We are also grateful that Kelley has made it available freely via Creative Commons for the use of scholars and business professionals.)

One reason design thinking has become so popular among business leaders is the radically and constantly increasing complexity of business today. We have already discussed how complicated and interconnected the modern enterprise is. Business assets have multiple owners often with competing agendas and varying views of risk. New risks, many of them unimaginable until very recently, are constantly emerging. And events very far away – a tsunami in Japan, political unrest in the Middle East, a ring of hackers working out of Russia – can have immediate impacts dangerously close to home. These complex, almost incomprehensible business environments call for an entirely new approach, and design thinking – while it's not the only one, by any means – is the one we've found most useful in our security careers.

## 5.1.1 The Phases of Design Thinking

The design thinking process is broken down into phases, as you can see from the model in Figure 5-1. It progresses through the steps of:

1. Empathy.
2. Definition.
3. Ideation.
4. Prototyping.
5. Testing.

In the next few sections we'll explore what is meant by each of those concepts.

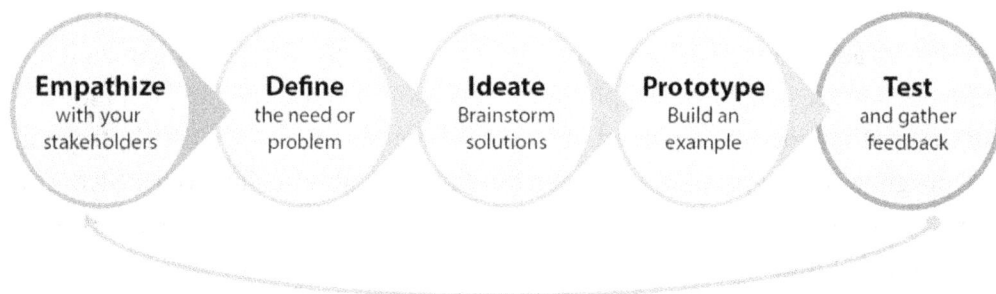

*Figure 5-1. The Design Thinking Process Begins with – and, Crucially, Returns to – Empathy. (Stanford University Institute of Design, 2013, p. 1)*

## 5.1.1.1 Empathy

*Empathy* is, at its core, the ability to understand and share the feelings of another person. It is something that is very important to literally every human being. We all feel the need to be listened to and understood, in business and our personal lives, in our classes and communities, when we are the consumer of a product or service, or the provider. Empathy allows us to get along better with our fellow human beings because we have the ability to put ourselves in their shoes and see things through their eyes.

In design thinking terms, empathy means recognizing the people who will be most impacted by whatever it is you are trying to accomplish (the stakeholders that you've already identified, and also other impacted groups like the general employee population, or supervisors who will have to enforce a new policy) and making a serious, honest attempt to understand what they need and want from you and your program – not just as strategic partners, *but as human beings.* Above all, it means *listening* (Stanford University Institute of Design, 2013, p. 1).

### Tasks of the Empathy Phase

1. Understand for yourself which process or aspect of the program you are redesigning.
2. Talk to people in your organization about how they feel about the current process.
3. Ask:
   - What can be improved?
   - What do they like about the current process?
   - How will changing the process or implementing a new process impact them?
4. LISTEN to your partners.
5. Understand their point of view.

## 5.1.1.2 Definition

In design thinking, *definition* means taking what you've learned from the empathy phase – what you've heard your strategic partners say about their wants and needs and about the challenges and other issues they're experiencing – and establishing your own view of the problem that needs to be solved (Stanford University Institute of Design, 2013, p. 2). Once you've done that, you can craft (define) an actionable statement that can be communicated effectively to everyone involved.

### Tasks of the Definition Phase

1. Review the results of your conversations in the empathy phase.
2. Review and redefine your own understanding of the issue at stake.
3. Clearly define the problem that needs to be solved in language that everyone can understand.

## 5.1.1.3 Ideation/Brainstorming

*Ideation* is the process of moving beyond identifying a problem to once again working with your partners and defining potential solutions (Stanford University Institute of Design, 2013, p. 3). This is a phase where it's absolutely essential not to limit your thinking, or anyone else's. Be as creative as possible – and encourage as much creativity as possible – so that you can generate a broad range of ideas, including some that may not be realistic at all.

### Tasks of the Ideation Phase

1. Set up brainstorming meetings with security personnel and stakeholders.
2. Clearly communicate the problem defined in the last step and look for solutions.
3. Accept all ideas – even "bad" ones.
4. Narrow the ideas down until you arrive at what seems like the best, most workable solution for everyone.

### 5.1.1.4 Prototyping

The *prototyping* phase is where you begin to build – whether in real life or virtually.

The prototype (sometimes called a pilot project) doesn't have to be polished, or even complete. It could be as simple as a storyboard or outline presentation that people can look at or "walk through" – and, crucially, provide feedback on as to how they feel it meets the needs that have been identified up to that point (Stanford University Institute of Design, 2013, p. 4).

If the prototype is more than just an on-paper design, and you decide to do a pilot, make it small, and involve stakeholders who have been part of the project all the way through. This way they are invested in making sure the process is workable for everyone.

#### Tasks of the Prototyping Phase

1. Build the model or template of the final process.
2. Present the model as a walk through to your stakeholder or run a limited pilot trial of the process.
3. Make sure your stakeholders have ample opportunity for feedback.

### 5.1.1.5 Testing

*Testing* in the design thinking model means actively soliciting feedback on your prototype – and actively listening to that feedback – and recognizing where it does and doesn't meet the needs that you and the other stakeholders have identified (Stanford University Institute of Design, 2013, p. 5).

#### Tasks of the Testing Phase

1. Allow the prototype to run for a set period of time.
2. Gather feedback from all stakeholders at the beginning, at set points along the way, and at the end of the test.
3. Modify the process or procedure based on the feedback from all parties.

And when these phases are complete? *The entire process begins again.* You circle directly back to the beginning of the process, returning to empathy (to understand how the people involved in the testing process feel about the prototype), definition (to confirm that your identification of the problem is correct), ideation (to identify potential changes that will solve the problem), and finally re-prototyping and re-testing. It is a continuous, ongoing cycle that will continue until you and the test stakeholders have reached agreement about the solution to the original security risk or problem.

### 5.2 Iterative ESRM Program Rollout in a Formal Design Thinking Model

When you're rolling out an ESRM program, it's critical to make the process as simple as possible. Security is a complex discipline, with a lot of moving parts, and you can't simply scrap your existing practices and start from scratch. (You can, however, reinvent and re-implement!) While the transition is taking place, the enterprise has to continue operating, and operating in a secure manner. You'll still have to perform all, or almost all, of the security tasks you were doing before. Access will still need to be controlled, investigations will still need to be conducted, and surveillance will still need to take place. The bottom line is that the security organization will still need to function, and function effectively, while you begin the transformation from security task management to security risk management.

That's why you need a clearly defined path, one that allows you to start with the core concepts and implement them; and then, once those are in place, expand the program to the next phase, and the next, until the entire program is moved into the ESRM way of managing security.

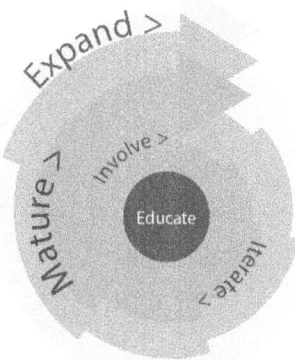

*Figure 5-2. Iterative Rollout Model*

The model shown in Figure 5-2 illustrates how you can use design thinking to implement your ESRM program in a phased approach. We'll use language that's slightly different here (including both design thinking terms and the terms in Figure 5-2) because the steps are specific to putting an ESRM program in place – Educate > Involve > Iterate > Mature > Expand (Repeat). But we'll also point out where in this expanding iterative process that the different "formal" design thinking pieces fit.

## 5.2.1 Educate and Involve (Empathy)

The first, and in some ways the most important, element of design thinking, is empathy. In rolling out your ESRM program, beginning with empathy means taking some very concrete steps:

First, you need to educate – starting with yourself and your security team, and then moving on to others in the business. We talked earlier about this step of stopping what you are doing and really understanding it. Understanding – by now that should sound very familiar, because we've been talking about this, in one way or another, since the beginning of this book. You need to understand your business, the risks, the assets, and the people responsible for those risks and assets – your stakeholders and your internal partners in protecting your enterprise. These are all steps you completed earlier in this book. Now, let's go further.

The step of understanding and educating yourself, which comes at the very beginning of the iterative process, is the most complex – and it's absolutely essential to your ESRM success. You must completely challenge your current security management and your current security practices. That means taking a step back and determining, of those current practices, what is true security risk management practice and what is not. You must identify those nuances, conducting a gap analysis for every process you perform, to find the difference between what it does and what it should be doing to meet your strategic partners' needs. You'll need to work to understand all those moving parts, and then add in an understanding of what they do for your stakeholders and how the processes mesh with what your stakeholders need and want from you.

In order to get that final piece of understanding of what they need and want, you'll need to work to educate with your strategic partners. Why? If you can't convince your key stakeholders of the value of your program, the implementation simply isn't going to happen, or at least isn't going to be successful. And your partners aren't going to understand the value of your program unless they understand and agree with the role of security in the company: that base understanding of the ESRM philosophy of who "owns" security risk (they do) vs. the role of security in identifying and helping them understand that risk. You can't be successful in your security management if you and your stakeholders don't first come to an agreement about what "success" is.

The need for your strategic partners to grasp the value of your program is why the essential second step in using iterative design thinking to roll out your ESRM program is to involve everyone who is touched by the program or may be part of it in the future, to identify those who need involvement and to communicate with them, clearly and effectively, throughout the process.

### 5.2.2 Iterate (Your Definition and Prototypes)

Here's where we begin to apply what we've learned from all those stakeholders about their wants and needs, and put into place ways of meeting them. Using design thinking, a product designer working on a new mobile phone might start with a mockup or a working model that shows the direction the project is going in. This is prototyping, and it can be applied just as easily, and just as effectively, to an ESRM program as it is to a product. As we discussed above, the rollout of the ESRM program can be done one process at a time, transitioning from simply a task your group does to an accepted and business-driven mitigation of a security risk that involves the appropriate asset owner in the process of determining the correct risk response. Each piece can be taken and reworked into a prototype process or policy that your stakeholder can step through and then provide feedback on.

Here's an example: As a security professional, you may have been tasked with securing a physical facility, and you're considering installing biometrics authentication – fingerprint readers – for all employees. But as you've talked with various stakeholders, you've heard concerns expressed about this approach being intrusive and possibly violating employees' privacy. One simple solution is to set up a pilot project (a prototype, in design terms) in one facility or one part of one facility. You may choose to make it an opt-in project, so that only employees who are comfortable with the program have to be involved. The result: You can find out whether the technology works, whether it's effective, and whether, in the long term, it will face significant resistance from the people involved. An added benefit: It lets you do all this without the cost of implementing a full-scale program that you might end up canceling. Once you have the small-scale prototype up and running, the feedback from your stakeholders will allow you to continue to refine the process until it's something that's acceptable and able to be fully rolled out (or perhaps unacceptable and not implemented – depending on the final decision of the asset/risk owner). The important thing is to start small, get feedback, make adjustments, and iterate and keep iterating until you've got it right.

### 5.2.3 Mature the Process (Testing/Feedback)

Maturing the process is the next piece in the ever-expanding circle in the iterative model. Remember, though, the human element (empathize/involve) doesn't disappear just because you've got your project under way, and you can't stop listening to the people impacted just because your prototype seems to be a success. This testing and feedback is part and parcel of design thinking. The feedback you get at the beginning of an implementation may change – more than once – as it goes on. People will begin to see different or better ways that things could work, and you need to take their changing perceptions for your program to reach full maturity.

The fact is, you aren't the one who can judge whether your process is a success – or at least you aren't the only one. Let's go back to our biometric authentication project. The technology is working, you're not seeing any glitches in the hardware or the software, and you're not hearing any complaints. But that's not good enough. You need to reach out, proactively and seriously, to everyone involved, to find out what they really think about having to have their fingerprints read to get to their workstations. They may not be complaining to the security guards, they may not be complaining to their managers (most people are understandably reluctant to do that), but that doesn't necessarily mean they're comfortable with what you're making them do. And the only way for you to know for sure is to engage with them, in a way that lets them know you're serious about their views.

### 5.2.4 Expand (Begin the Design Thinking Process Again with a Larger Scope)

If you follow the process as we've outlined it, each project you do will eventually come to the point where it's mature and running smoothly. At that point, it's time to expand your scope into another area – to bring another process into the ESRM model. When you do that, you're expanding the ESRM program as a whole. That can mean expanding to other locations, addressing other types of risk, or working with an entirely new set of stakeholders. It may also (and it probably should) mean raising ESRM's profile within the enterprise, so that senior executives and other high-level decision-makers are beginning to recognize the business value of the program and are willing to consider applying it in other areas. The key is that each round is made up of exactly the same steps. You start back with education and involvement, ensuring that you use empathy to understand the people involved, then iterate your designs and prototypes, and finally mature the new aspect of the program through feedback. This is why our model diagram is an ever-expanding spiral of the same steps. It keeps going, getting larger and larger as you engage more stakeholders, bring in more processes, identify more risks to mitigate, and build more and more partnerships.

So where does the design thinking cycle end? Okay, we admit it: That's a trick question. It doesn't. Not ever. It's a continuous, ongoing cycle of listening, learning, trying new things – sometimes successful, sometimes failures, sometimes a mix of the two – and using what you've learned to mature and expand. And it never stops.

## 5.3 ESRM Program Rollout Checklist

So far in, we've talked a lot about models and examples, walked you through diagrams and cycles, and discussed what we've done in the past and how we would do it now. By this point, we hope you have a flavor of the different ways you might approach this same process in your own organization. But we can almost hear you thinking out loud right now: "Okay, but what do I do…?" So we're including a checklist in Table 5-1 of steps for you to use in rolling out your own program. The principles of this approach are clear and consistent. Success will be driven by a multistep approach consisting of many small steps, not a few big ones. We recommend all of them, but by now, if you've followed our advice so far, you understand your enterprise and its needs and can tailor the checklist to fit your rollout.

**Table 5-1. ESRM Rollout Checklist**

| Phase | Action/Step |
|---|---|
| <ul><li>Empathy.</li><li>Educate (yourself).</li><li>Understand (your existing program).</li><li>Challenge current notions of security.</li></ul> | 1. STOP.<br>  a. Take a step back, and examine your program and what you're doing.<br>  b. Challenge your current notions of what security is.<br>  c. Understand the existing situation.<br>2. List all the security tasks you manage.<br>  a. Tie the existing parts of your program to definite business/asset owners and stakeholders.<br>  b. Identify the security risk the tasks are mitigating.<br>  c. Identify the owners of those risks.<br>  d. For each task, determine if it's operating under a risk management model, according to the principles outlined in this book.<br>3. Set the stage.<br>  a. Envision what the program would look like if you applied ESRM principles to all your processes.<br>  b. Consider what steps you would take to execute ESRM throughout the program. |

| | |
|---|---|
| | c. Identify whom you would need to engage and how they might respond to the idea of ESRM.<br><br>d. Strategize around hurdles you may face and a plan to take them on. Be ready with responses to anticipated challenges about the ESRM philosophy. |
| • Define (in agreement with your partners) what the enterprise needs from security.<br>• Educate (your partners).<br>• Involve (business executives). | 1. Discuss.<br>  a. Explore the idea of ESRM with your close co-workers outside of security, getting comfortable with the terminology, hearing their counterpoints, and understanding what they may or may not agree with.<br>  b. Identify key line-of-business executives who are critical for success. Explore the ESRM practice with them and how it would benefit their goals. Start with trusted strategic partners. Start simple and get everybody on the same page.<br>2. Present.<br>  a. Meet with the highest level of executive you can reach. CEO is the best place to start, of course. If that's not possible, start as high as you can get in your organizational structure, and make that person aware of the need to take this discussion as high as it can go.<br>  b. Explain the philosophy of ESRM (see section 9 of this book – What Do Executives Need to Know About ESRM? – for an executive-friendly format for doing this).<br>  c. Explain the role of security in managing – not owning – risk.<br>  d. Get the executive to agree with you that the role of security in the organization is to identify risks to business assets and work with those asset owners to respond to those risks, either through a mitigation program, or by acceptance by the person with the necessary authority. *(Note: If you can't get this philosophical agreement, the ESRM program isn't going to get very far. It's a relatively "easy sell," if you point out the business risks and the ESRM methodologies we lay out in this book. But if you don't get the agreement you need, keep trying – with that same person in another round with more backup* |

<table>
<tr>
<td></td>
<td>

*information, or with a different person of influence who might be able to advance the ESRM cause.)*

    e. Once you have agreement, make sure you continually stress and explain your role in every interaction with the executive, until it becomes ingrained in his or her perception of you and your organization that your role is to point out and manage risk in partnership with the business asset and risk owners.

3. Document.

    a. Develop a written security policy based on ESRM that outlines the agreed upon role of security and ensure it's endorsed by the executives in charge.

4. Charter a security council (more on that later) to govern the ESRM program and help drive adoption.

</td>
</tr>
<tr>
<td>

- Brainstorm and prototype.
- Develop an outline of the essentials of a program.
- Test and engage stakeholders.
- Incorporate feedback and iterate with changes.

</td>
<td>

1. Take it one step at a time.
2. Start with a program or a part of an existing program developing a strategy on how to implement the ESRM practice. Invite stakeholders into those strategy sessions.

*Note: For each aspect of your program, pick a process or standard that can be converted to an ESRM model. Here are the basic steps to take for any particular process or procedure to be brought into the ESRM model.*

3. Prototype the process.

    a. Involve your strategic partners who are most impacted and involved with the process you are rolling out and brainstorm with them and team members on where to start in creating an environment that would engage stakeholders.

    b. Work through a prototype of a program from scratch. Some of the current program may fit right into ESRM, but it's important to identify why they fit.

    c. Identify what processes and steps would be different in the prototype and what the program would look like moving forward, even if they are just nuances. The nuances you'll find are incredibly important.

    d. Educate the team and stakeholders on the prototype and anticipate challenges. Focus on the long term benefits and beyond individual programs or projects.

</td>
</tr>
</table>

| | |
|---|---|
| | e.   Ensure the model is repeatable and adaptable.<br>4.  Don't forget the details.<br>    a.   Start with the mission and goals. Break down the goals for process incorporating the ESRM principles.<br>    b.   Incorporate the practice into roles and responsibilities.<br>    c.   Assess current skillsets and job descriptions to see if they fit the program and personnel have the skills to be successful. |
| •  Iterate and expand.<br>•  Develop goals.<br>•  Integrate into roles and responsibilities.<br>•  Reinforce. | 1.  Listen and respond.<br>    a.   Make sure to build in a feedback process sticking to the agreed upon the ESRM philosophy. The business and security practice will fit into the ESRM practice if applied appropriately.<br>2.  Implement the process.<br>    a.   Pick a date to start using the new process in daily work.<br>    b.   Announce the change and ensure all strategic partners know exactly when it is starting.<br>    c.   Seek feedback from executives, impacted business units, and security practitioners outside your organization and iterated on the methodology and practice.<br>3.  Keep going!<br>    a.   Consistently reinforce the ESRM principles through education, conversation and program maturity.<br>    b.   Expand the practice into strategy and program development.<br>    c.   Pick a new process, procedure, or aspect of your program and begin another round of ESRM implementation. |

# Part 3

# Ensuring Long-Term ESRM Success

**This part will help you to:**

- ➤ Understand what elements are necessary for long-term success of your ESRM program.
- ➤ Ensure the proper governance of the security function in your enterprise.
- ➤ Explain the value of security and ESRM to executives using useful metrics and reports.

# 6

# Essentials for Success

Security is, of course, not the only enterprise function that addresses risks. We discussed the differences between ERM and ESRM earlier this book, and from there you learned that the enterprise risk department is one example of a risk-based function outside of security. Others include the internal audit, fraud investigations, and compliance organizations. All of these groups deal with their own types of risks, and deal with them in ways that will be familiar to the security professional – especially the security professional working in an ESRM model. And yet, the security organization doesn't always receive the level of respect and authority that those other risk-oriented functions do. No business executive would, for example, ever question an auditor's need to operate freely, without interference from the management of the groups that he or she is auditing or investigating, but the same executives wouldn't necessarily think of security in the same way.

Many security organizations report into IT, facilities, corporate services, or sometimes even operational organizations, and those reporting arrangements can often lead to conflicts. (Later we'll discuss best practices for organizational reporting structures for security, but for now, bear in mind that those structures we just listed aren't always optimal.) The risk-based management of security can only be truly successful if senior management recognizes and respects the security organization's similarities to these other risk-oriented functions – and recognizes that it has the same need for freedom of action that those functions receive.

In this section, we'll be discussing several essential foundational elements of a successful ESRM program:

- Transparency in identifying all risks, and communicating those risks and their root causes to all appropriate parties.
- Independence in making risks transparent, and when necessary escalating improper risk acceptance decisions.
- Authority of the security department's role.
- Scope of responsibility.

As a security professional designing and implementing an ESRM program, you'll need a comprehensive understanding of the role each of these foundational elements plays in the success of the program, and be able to explain their importance to others, in business terms – not technical or "security" terms. That's why this chapter focuses on the factors that are essential to ESRM success.

That's also why we'll draw parallels between ESRM and other business-critical risk-based functions, like audit and compliance. Audit and compliance professionals operate in a risk-management model, and those groups have been managing their non-security types of risks (financial, policy, ethics) in that fashion long enough that their need for transparency, independence, authority, and proper scope is now well-understood by business leaders. Drawing these parallels is important to ensure that your executives fully understand the need for the foundational elements for managing security risks as well, so after the discussion of the individual elements, we'll include a short discussion of similarities between security, as practiced in the ESRM model, and other functions as they relate to each of those elements: transparency, independence, authority, and scope.

## 6.1 Transparency

Few concepts are as central to ESRM – and ESRM success – as *transparency*. (It's also central to those other risk-based functions we were talking about earlier. Nobody would expect an auditing organization to do an effective job if the organization being audited were not open and honest, and the reverse is also true – the auditors must be equally open and honest about what they're doing.) As we've seen already, the ESRM philosophy is based fundamentally on collaboration and cooperation with business asset and risk owners and other stakeholders. We as security professionals can't expect our strategic partners in the enterprise to make a serious commitment to long-term working relationships with us if we aren't open and honest and clear with them about we're doing, why we're doing it, and what we need from them. That's what we mean by transparency. Transparency takes many forms, but in ESRM terms, it has two key dimensions: process transparency and risk transparency.

### 6.1.1 Process Transparency

When you're managing security risks, and the security risk process, being transparent about the entire decision-making process – how you arrived at your recommendations to the risk owners, and why, and the possible outcomes if those recommendations are accepted – is a critical part of your role. In ESRM terms, this *process transparency* means:

- Being open and honest about real security risks, neither exaggerating them to get a project approved nor minimizing them for "political" reasons.
- Ensuring that all impacted parties are aware of a given risk and participate in discussions about accepting or mitigating that risk.
- Exploring all the elements of a risk, not simply the obvious, superficial aspects.
- Offering risk treatment options commensurate with the level of risk.
- Receiving and documenting – in writing – the risk owner's final decision on the mitigation or acceptance of the risk.

These straightforward principles offer real value to everyone involved in security risk decisions. They'll protect you and everyone else, inside and outside the security organization, against finger-pointing and "blame-shifting." That's because they ensure that risk and risk ownership are clearly defined, the person making the decision is the right one, and that person is fully accountable for the outcome.

If the security risk management process doesn't have the right degree of transparency, you and the security organization may be accused of not managing the risk process appropriately. More importantly, that may well be true, with serious consequences for the enterprise. That's because, by not being transparent or not involving the right people, you could be facilitating the acceptance of a risk that shouldn't be accepted, or the mitigation of one that doesn't really require mitigation. And there's another problem: A lack of transparency may alienate key stakeholders – stakeholders whose cooperation and collaboration you may need in the future. Remember how we discussed empathy in your program design and rollout? It didn't end there.

Let's use the example of an online gift basket company: Gwendolen's Online Gifts.

### Case Study: The Problem of a Stakeholder Who Was Excluded

Gwendolen's Online Gifts (GOG) is a fast-growing online retailer that creates and ships customized gift baskets. The company has two security managers, each with a separate, clearly defined set of responsibilities. Jessica H., the information security manager, is charged with risks related to the company's digital systems, which are obviously mission-critical, while Cynthia W., the corporate security manager, is tasked with operational and physical security risks.

The company's rapid growth is placing serious strains on GOG's order processing and fulfillment capacity. One day over lunch, John C., the director in charge of the customer care organization, tells Jessica in passing about a plan to increase order-handling capacity cost-effectively by outsourcing to a third-party call center in Ireland. Jessica immediately recognizes that exposing customer information to a third party represents a security risk, and tells John she will need to conduct a security assessment before any contract is signed.

Jessica's team looks at the outsourcer's information security policies and procedures, checks its technical standards, and even had the company agree to penetration testing of its network. When the outsourcing project is announced to the entire leadership group, Jessica reports to the VP of operations that the call center can be trusted to handle GOG's customer data. It seems like all is well.

But in terms of interpersonal, or "political," concerns, all is not well. After the meeting, Cynthia takes Jessica aside and asks why she was not included in the assessment. Jessica replies that since Cynthia is in charge of onsite physical and operational security, and the outsourced call center is not part of that, she did not think it was necessary to bring her in. But Cynthia disagrees, saying she had, and has, some concerns about the project – and it is clear that she is not happy.

At first, Jessica is bewildered by Cynthia's reaction. After all, she took a close look at the potential risks to the company's customer data, and found all the technical protections more than adequate. But as she gives it more thought, she realizes that she did not think much about the actual physical protections around the data center, the background checks of personnel, or even the physical access control. She understood why Cynthia was upset, and assured her that the next time an assessment was done, she would bring Cynthia in as a partner in the risk process.

In the case study above, we saw Jessica complete a security assessment, but really she only assessed the security risks associated with the tasks she managed in her department's area of expertise – the risks she was responsible for the mitigation of. This means that although she told the business function leaders that a full security risk assessment had been done and passed, she in fact did not fully explore the risks associated with the outsourcing project. She did not make sure all the appropriate stakeholders were informed, aware, and involved. She was not transparent about the process – and the result was that, in effect, she accepted a risk that was not her's to accept.

Transparency about the security and risk process – especially opening it up for discussion before a final decision is made – makes for better risk mitigation and acceptance decisions, and protects the security professional against finger-pointing when things go wrong. Even when things don't go wrong, it helps prevent hard feelings from stakeholders who feel they should have been involved and were not – hard feelings that can make future projects far more difficult than they need to be.

By making security risk management process transparent to all the appropriate parties, you allow – and in fact encourage – everyone impacted by the process to have their say. Now, some of those stakeholders may disagree with your viewpoint or your recommendations. Not only is there nothing wrong with that, it's actually very healthy, because it exposes concerns you may not have identified and introduces ideas you may not have considered.

A lack of process transparency represents a fundamental flaw in the risk assessment. This is because it can lead to individuals who should be brought into the process, or who at least have more information about the risk, being left out of the risk treatment planning. And remember, under ESRM principles, you as the security professional are never the risk owner. If you don't bring in the proper asset or risk owners for signoff, you're essentially accepting at least part of the risk yourself – and that's not likely to end well.

Of course, as with any decision-making process in business, there have to be limits on how many people can be brought in. You'll need to balance the need for broad input with the need to actually get things done – making decisions, avoiding overanalyzing, and not wasting time and resources. Not all of those inclusion decisions will be easy ones, but making them, and getting them right, will be critical to your success and the success of your ESRM program.

## 6.1.2 Risk Transparency
The second critical dimension of transparency is *risk transparency*. As you progress through your career, you'll almost certainly come across security practitioners who – as strange as it may

sound – don't want security risks exposed. Maybe they're afraid of the repercussions of having risks exposed because they feel that pointing out a risk somehow makes it "their fault." Or maybe they simply want to make security decisions themselves, without consulting all impacted parts of the enterprise and all impacted stakeholders. Whatever their reasons, these people and their lack of transparency represent a serious threat to the maturity and success of your ESRM program. Let's be absolutely clear about this: As a security professional conducting an ESRM program, you're responsible for transparently reporting security risks to impacted company assets. If you fail to report to an asset owner and any other impacted parties that a real risk exists to a given asset, you are depriving those stakeholders of the opportunity to make a business decision about that risk.

The resistance to risk transparency is a common problem, and isn't limited to the security organization, by any means. Sometimes you'll also run into strategic partners (maybe we should make that "partners" in this case) who don't want to involve others in "their" risk assessment and treatment decisions. Maybe they're in a hurry, or maybe they think it's "just not that big a deal," or maybe they just think it's simpler not to find risks because risks create work. Resistance can also be driven by embarrassment. The exposed risk, if it costs the business money or slows down production, may make the manager feel like this could have been identified earlier in the process, making them look bad. It really doesn't matter *why* they take this attitude that limits the enterprise's ability to make sound risk decisions.

What *does* matter is what you do in response to that. It's critical that you stick to ESRM principles, demanding transparency and, of course, educating others on its importance. Of course arguing with a stubborn business stakeholder is difficult and unpleasant. You'll need to pick your battles, and you'll need to understand going in that you won't always win. In the real world, it's possible that a risk won't always be dealt with appropriately, and the outcome may not be a good one. But if you apply ESRM principles of risk transparency, at minimum, you'll have evidence that you've carried out your responsibilities. One of the most important and effective ways of ensuring transparency is explicit, formal, security policy that's documented and clearly understood by all stakeholders. This policy can literally be as simple and basic as the statement that anyone who sees a security issue is required to report it to the security organization. What matters is that there be no confusion on anyone's part about what is expected and required.

Transparency – around both process and risk – is a good benchmark for the maturity of your ESRM program. The greater your transparency across both these dimensions, and the greater the transparency you're able to get your strategic partners to commit to, the more successful your program will be.

## 6.2 Independence

Another critical component of ESRM success is independence in your security practice. One of the fundamental principles of ESRM is the need to have many different stakeholders involved in security risk decisions, and as we've already seen, those stakeholders often have competing, even contradictory, agendas and interests. That can translate into pressure to change – sometimes in subtle ways, sometimes blatantly – the assessments and recommendations you make concerning security risks. And that makes independence absolutely essential. The security organization must have the freedom to point out any security risks across the enterprise, without the fear of obstruction or retaliation from the leaders of the organization or function where that risk exists. It's the same principle that doesn't allow an internal audit team to report to an organization it might have to audit someday.

When you're managing enterprise security risks in any area – cybersecurity, information security, investigations, or crisis management – independence will enable you to manage the security practice without interference or pressure that could limit risk transparency. It's extremely important that you have "reach" into the entire enterprise, so that you can look into security vulnerabilities wherever they exist, understand the business and the business' assets, and, when responding to an incident, clearly identify its root causes. And it's obviously important that you be able to accomplish this without the threat of retaliation or other negative repercussions when you're simply doing your job.

There are plenty of reasons business partners might resist your efforts to identify and expose security vulnerabilities and security risks. They may view a security threat as a weakness in their management or their processes, and they may be worried that others – including their superiors – may see it that way. And, while we hope you never encounter this, they may be deliberately doing something that's against the enterprise's interests. In cases like these, the business partner may pressure you not to expose the risk or its root cause, possibly threatening you or your future career prospects, either directly or indirectly. Now imagine that that individual is in charge of your organization, or otherwise in a position of influence over you? What do you think would happen to either your risk assessment, or even your job, if that person truly wanted to keep a risk hidden? If you have a truly independent reporting structure, there is much less chance of this kind of pushback having an adverse impact on you and your career.

Let's look below at two examples of why independence is essential for your success in ESRM.

### Case Study: The Costs of Lack of Independence -- 1

Geri H. works as a security manager in the western region of a financial services company called Stalbridge. The company is highly competitive, and its salespeople, their managers, and all of the company's executives are compensated primarily based on the closing sales of various financial instruments. Geri reports into the regional services group which ultimately reports up through the finance organization to the company's senior vice president of the western region. Recently, Geri's counterpart in the southern region called her to make her aware that some salespeople there were taking advantage of a loophole in the change order process to fraudulently inflate their sales numbers and earn higher commissions. Geri began an investigation and found strong evidence that a number of salespeople in her region were doing the same.

Geri brought the results of her investigation to the sales manager responsible for those employees, expecting to be commended and to see those employees fired immediately.

> Instead, the next day, she received a call from the VP of Finance, Kevin T., telling her to stop the investigation, because exposing it would mean restating the results for the quarter and he needed to have those numbers in order to remain as the number one region in the company. He made it clear that the president of the region wouldn't like to lose that place, and that it would be a serious, even career-ending, mistake for Geri to make him unhappy.
>
> Eventually, Geri decided that her ethics were more important than one job and escalated the issue to Stalbridge's general counsel, Stanley M. Stanley immediately grasped the seriousness of the issue and ensured that the investigation went forward, now however, not only into those employees who had been inflating their numbers, but also into what levels of management might have been complicit. Escalating the issue outside of her reporting structure to Stanley was a gamble on Geri's part. She did not know whether the reaction would be to commend her or fire her. After this incident, Stanley decided that he would bring the investigations function into his group to prevent a situation like that ever happening again.

Now, a situation like the one described at Stalbridge places the security practitioner in an extremely difficult position. She's been given a direct order, from someone in her own reporting structure who has a strong personal, professional – and, yes, financial – interest in the security issue. Now, while there are almost certainly other, competing interests, like shareholder liability and fraud reporting requirements, Kevin's decision is clearly based entirely on his own interests. His compensation and possibly even his current and future positions in this company depend on those sales numbers. Geri knows the right thing to do, the thing called for by company policy, is to conduct a more thorough investigation. If she doesn't do that, she could be accused of sweeping a serious problem under the rug. But if she does do it, she may be threatening her own career. She's caught between a rock and a hard place – but if she had a clear and independent reporting structure, she wouldn't be. Stanley saw that and fixed the problem, granting Geri the independent reporting structure her job required.

Our second example comes from the IT world.

## Case Study: The Costs of Lack of Independence -- 2

Sean L. is the information security manager for VitaCorp, a small chain of pharmacies. He reports into the IT organization. The CIO, Adrienne F., wants to implement a new software application that is expected to save the retail ordering group several million dollars over the next seven years. Time is of the essence, because Adrienne has promised sales, finance, and operating executives that the application will be up and running in just two months. When Sean reviews the project, he identifies a number of significant security vulnerabilities that could expose customer data. Those vulnerabilities need to be studied – and possibly mitigated – and that is what he tells Adrienne. Adrienne's response: The vulnerabilities are unlikely to impact the project, and there's no time for further study. The project is moving forward without further discussion or proper risk acceptance.

An organizational structure like the one at VitaCorp that has IT security reporting to IT represents an inherent, obvious conflict of interest, one that threatens the security professional's needed independence. Most IT projects have tight budgets and timelines, and those demands are often driven by executives – powerful ones – outside the IT structure. In this example,

Adrienne's financial incentives are likely based on her performance in executing against her budget and implementing the project commitments she's made. Her insistence on pushing the project through is understandable, as is Sean's reluctance to see it happen. But an information security manager has very little independence here. If you, as an IT security professional, have identified a major security vulnerability that would significantly slow up a major project and potentially impact the CIO's appearance of success, would you feel comfortable escalating that risk outside of your chain of command? Most people – including Sean – would not.

There's another issued to be considered here, from the ESRM point of view. As you've already learned, it's critical to identify the true owner of the asset under consideration. Many times, even in IT projects, the IT risk is not the CIO's risk to accept. In this example, to make appropriate risk recommendations, Sean would need to know what data was being used in the new system, and who had a vested interest in ensuring the security of that data – he'd have to make the decision to escalate the issue to those stakeholders, effectively going over Adrienne's head. Not a very good position to be in, is it?

In both of the situations we've described in our examples, an independent reporting structure would have helped the security practitioner avoid both conflicts of interest and potential repercussions. And if the structures had been independent from the outset, the problems would have been much less likely to occur in the first place, because the business leader would have known that a reporting line was in place that would allow the security practitioner to escalate any threats or acts of retaliation.

## 6.3 Authority

Managing a security department with transparency and independence carries with it an extraordinary amount of authority – authority that needs to be respected and used properly. Authority is extremely important to the entire ESRM process, but it must not be abused in any way, for any reason. That's because ESRM success depends in large measure on building partnerships between the security organization and other business units. This is important, and beneficial to all involved, but it can sometimes feel threatening to people and organizations that may not be accustomed to this type of working relationship. Simply by having the kind of access and the purpose of identifying security risks, exposing those security risks, and helping to manage the mitigation planning process, you reach into another organization, and that can feel like a threat to some business leaders.

### Case Study: Why Authority Matters

Diana P. works as a security manager at Finehart Home Theater, an installer of top-of-the-line, custom, home electronics systems. Her security function reports up into the facilities group. Recently, Diana has been following a high-profile local news story: a sexual assault case involving another local retailer, Appliance Galaxy. An Appliance Galaxy employee has been accused of attacking a customer in her home while making a delivery. The police investigation has revealed that the employee has a criminal record for a similar offense. The result has been an avalanche of bad publicity – and threats of lawsuits – for Appliance Galaxy.

Diana realizes that Finehart could easily find itself in a similar situation, so she approaches the installations manager, Susan G., to discuss the possibility of doing background checks on installers. Susan tells her that none of her installers would ever be a problem, because she hires them all personally and knows how to read people. And besides, finding skilled technicians is hard enough already. Why would she want to add an extra layer of difficulty to the process? She makes it clear that she has no intention of making any changes.

Diana describes the conversation to her boss, the director of facilities, Harold B., who reminds her that nothing like the Appliance Galaxy incident has ever happened at Finehart, so Susan "must be doing something right." And he adds, "We are facilities, what are we supposed to do? Just drop it." Diana is frustrated, and she's still very concerned, but there's no one left in the company for her to turn to – at least not without risking her job – so she moves on to her next project and hopes for the best.

In the Finehart story, Diana clearly doesn't have the authority to escalate inappropriate risk acceptance in the organization. Rather than take the risk of going outside of her chain of command, Diana dropped the issue. Hoping for the best is not the most effective risk mitigation strategy, and an ESRM risk-based approach would have given Diana the ability to continue to pursue the background check issue with the appropriate defense that she was fulfilling security's role of exploring all company security risk.

A note on the authority aspect of having a successful security program: the very necessary authority that comes from an effective ESRM program can – and should – make you feel empowered to do your job thoroughly and effectively, but it can also damage a security organization and destroy a career if it isn't used wisely. The application of ESRM principles provides guidance and structure to your process and workflow, ensuring that everyone involved sees how you're working and that no abuses of authority are occurring. So if it seems threatening to some people that you're "in their business," looking for and exposing risks, you can help them to understand that it's really a collaborative process, and that it's there to help protect them, too.

Of course, no matter how much authority you have, you still need to manage security risk using the ESRM principles we've already discussed to be fully protected from possible retaliation. Why? Because when you're managing security risk through the use of fundamental risk principles and someone tries to bury or avoid the risk through intimidation or retaliation, your defense – which is both honest and effective – is that you were simply trying to manage the security risk according to a predefined and accepted process. A business leader who tried to influence the outcome inappropriately would be shown as not following the process. But the same applies to you as the security practitioner. If you were the one trying to use your implied authority to push through a security risk mitigation decision, you'd be giving your business partner good reason to push back on you and the process – and the conversation would be about you and your decision-making, *not* about the risk. And remember, when you're applying ESRM principles, the risk response decision isn't yours to make, anyway. The ESRM process – transparent and independent and collaborative – is where you make your contribution.

## 6.4 Scope

The final aspect of ESRM success that we need to consider is scope – the extent and the limits of your work in managing security risks. What should be the scope of your ESRM program? The answer varies somewhat depending on the department, the individual, and what the business feels is important – we'll go back to the understanding and exploration phase you've already gone through. You ought to have a good idea at the end of that process of what your scope *should* be, and be able to articulate that as you set up your ESRM program. Your *role* remains the same: to manage security risks of all types across the enterprise through the use of risk principles – within whatever your defined scope of program responsibility is.

As we've seen, however, program scope is sometimes perceived and defined in terms of the security organization's tasks or the individual security practitioner's responsibilities, rather than the program's working philosophy and goals of managing the security risk process enterprise-wide. Plenty of security managers' program scope could be summed up by the phrase "whatever my boss tells me to do" or "other duties as assigned." That's scope defined by tasks and task management – and it's definitely not ESRM. An example would be limiting the scope of the security risk managed by the program only to risks that could impact the tangible assets of buildings because the most visible tasks performed by the personnel in the current security group are camera management and identification badges. Scope simply cannot be predefined as "what the security group is already doing" when implementing your overarching ESRM program.

This does not imply that the tasks performed by security personnel are not influenced by scope or do not have a place in ESRM. Those *activities* that an ESRM-based security program performs for the business may be very similar to those a task-management-based organization performs on a day-to-day basis.

But the scope of the security organization's responsibilities in an ESRM environment is different. In ESRM, the reason for performing day-to-day security tasks is in service of risk management, not just a job description. All security tasks are taken on in response to specific, identified, and prioritized risks to organization assets. They are risk mitigation actions that are *accepted and signed off by the business* – and *then* assigned to the subject-matter experts in security to carry out. It is a subtle difference, but an important one.

### 6.4.1 Example: Risk Management in Scope with Mitigation Actions by Security

One obvious security risk that needs to be managed for a data center is the possibility of an unauthorized person stealing or maliciously compromising valuable enterprise data. As a security manager operating under ESRM principles, you would identify and prioritize this risk with the asset owners, and you would likely recommend mitigating the risk with access controls, both physical and logical. In many organizations, the security department would probably also end up performing the actual *task* of implementing and managing those access controls, because that is the group that has personnel with the necessary skills.

It's important not to assume that the security department will always be carrying out the mitigation tasks. Sometimes, the tasks associated with mitigating a risk will not fall to the security department because it will not be in the area of security expertise.

### 6.4.2 Example: Risk Management in Scope with Mitigation Actions by the Business

An example of a risk that is in the scope of the ESRM to manage, but not mitigate, is another relatively obvious risk – the risk of fraud in a commission-based sales environment. In this example, we will say you once again work with your colleagues in sales to identify risk, and you recommend controls that could be put into business processes that would reduce the risk of fraudulent activity. However, those business processes belong to the sales group. In this mitigation plan, it is their task to make sure the processes are in place and functioning to reduce the risk of fraud.

The critical distinction here is that the *scope* of an ESRM program can include identifying, prioritizing, and managing mitigation plans for security risks, *even if the security organization does not perform the mitigation tasks.*

So here's what *program scope* means in ESRM terms:

> ➢ All of the risks your organization is managing *in partnership* with other internal organizations.

Now, we can't define that scope for you. You'll have to do that yourself, and with your organization's leadership, as you work to understand the business and identify stakeholders – the process we mentioned at the beginning of this section. Some enterprises may already have clearly defined scope for certain areas; for example, making fraud the responsibility of the security team but assigning violations of company policy to the compliance department. You're the one who knows your enterprise, and as you apply ESRM principles, you'll get to know it even better. That knowledge will make it possible for you to fully understand the scope of your ESRM responsibilities, so that you can effectively manage all the risks within that scope.

You and your program may not always have the scope that's necessary and appropriate for you to carry out your responsibilities with complete effectiveness, at least not at the outset. There will always be issues – like inappropriate job titles and descriptions and confused or "siloed" (isolated) organizational structures – that will make the process of defining and establishing scope more difficult. Practicing ESRM doesn't mean you'll necessarily get – or that you should necessarily push for – increased scope of responsibilities. Your organization may have silos of responsibility for excellent reasons. But if you use ESRM principles, there don't have to be any inherent limits on program scope, and the more effectively you apply ESRM principles, the more likely it will be that you're given the scope you need in the context of your organization.

Even if some mitigation plans or risks are outside the scope of your program, one advantage of ESRM principles is that you can still interact with the other groups that do have ownership of certain risks and know that your discussions will be centered only on the management of those risks. As a result, you will be much less likely to appear to be attempting to enlarge your sphere of responsibility at the expense of another group. You will simply be engaging in a very appropriate and necessary discussion of what mitigations are in place for identified security risks.

# 7

# ESRM Governance, Metrics, and Reporting

Executive oversight and support of the security program are critical to ensuring an appropriate department structure in the enterprise, which in turn is the key to maintaining those foundational aspects we discussed above – transparency, independence, authority, and scope. Without those, your ability to properly identify risks and the appropriate risk owners, and to work with them on risk mitigation plans is compromised. A formal governance structure in the form of a documented policy, governance program, and executive security council is the final link in the chain tying together all of the pieces we have discussed so far, and your key to making certain that the needed executive support and oversight are in place.

## 7.1 What is Corporate Governance?

The best starting point in developing an understanding of ESRM governance is to recognize that it's a subset of a broader concept, one that is of critical and growing importance in the business world: corporate governance. Corporate governance is essentially the set of systems and processes that a well-managed company puts in place to ensure that it acts appropriately in its relations with all of its stakeholders. Those stakeholders may include its shareholders if it's a publicly traded company, its customers, its employees, its industry partners, vendors, even the larger community. (**Note:** Even though we're referring here to corporate governance, the same principles apply – sometimes even more strictly – to public-sector entities and nonprofit organizations.) Why is this so important? Because, as a glance at the newspaper headlines shows us on a nearly daily basis, not taking corporate governance seriously can be extremely damaging to your company – its reputation, its brand, and its bottom line.

Just looking back a few years, we can see a number of names that were brought into household prominence because of scandals involving fraud, corruption, or other corporate governance issues. Below is a quick snapshot of some of the scandals caused in part by poor corporate governance. How many of these stories are familiar to you? Some names will live on in infamy for decades to come; some, the companies would be happy for you to forget.

- 2015 – The Volkswagen emissions scandal – in which the auto manufacturer admits installing software on its diesel vehicles to misrepresent their pollution standards – costs the company roughly $20 million in market value.

- 2015 – The electronics manufacturer is found to have overstated its profits by $1.9 billion. The company's CEO resigns, and Japanese regulators recommend a $60 million fine.
- 2014 – The Chinese government fines the pharmaceutical firm GlaxoSmithKline $489 million for paying doctors to use its drugs.
- 2013 – The collapse of a textile factory in Dhaka, Bangladesh – used to manufacture clothing for brands including JCPenney – kills at least 1,130 workers.
- 2012 – Barclays and other leading banks are implicated in a scheme to manipulate the London Inter-Bank Offered Rate (LIBOR), an exchange rate that is crucial to honest dealings between banks. The chief executive officer (CEO) and chief operating officer (COO) of Barclays, among other leading financial industry figures, are forced to resign.
- 2012 – At least eight senior Walmart executives, including the company's chief administrative officer, leave the company following accusations of widespread bribery in Mexico.
- 2011 – News Corp, parent company of Fox News, faces criminal and civil charges into accusations of phone hacking.

Corporate governance has many different formal definitions – but there are a few basic principles that are generally agreed on:

- Transparency.
- Accountability.
- Fairness.
- Responsibility.

(These should sound familiar. They're essentially the same concepts we talked about earlier as the basics of a successful ESRM program.) These are core principles for any business today, and they are core concepts that your strategic partners in the enterprise are deeply concerned with. That's why we're going to discuss corporate governance, and its applications to ESRM, in detail here.

### 7.1.1 Why Corporate Governance Is Complex

One reason corporate governance is so complex is that there are so many different factors that influence it: laws, regulations, industry standards, accepted best practices, and more. These factors vary widely, from country to country, from region to region, and from industry to industry. The US, for example, defines and mandates some aspects of corporate governance through the financial transparency requirements of the Sarbanes-Oxley Act of 2002. (You'll sometimes hear it referred to as just Sarbanes-Oxley, Sarbox, or SOX.) The European Union (EU) has its own corporate governance requirements. But there's no single international standard that all countries and all industries are required, or even expected, to follow (Dowdney, 2005).

## 7.1.2 Importance of OECD Guidelines

There is, however, one very influential set of guidelines that, even though it's nonbinding, offers a solid foundation for an understanding of corporate governance. These guidelines were developed by the Organisation for Economic Co-operation and Development (OECD), an international policy organization with 34 member countries that either adopt its guidelines or use them as a basis for their own regulations and laws (Organisation for Economic Co-operation and Development, 2015). The OECD is extremely influential, even beyond its member countries, and its *Principles of Corporate Governance* (published in 1999 and revised in 2004) are widely accepted.

On their web site, the OECD defines *corporate governance* as:

> Procedures and processes according to which an organisation is directed and controlled. The corporate governance structure specifies the distribution of rights and responsibilities among the different participants in the organisation – such as the board, managers, shareholders and other stakeholders – and lays down the rules and procedures for decision-making. (Organisation for Economic Co-operation and Development, 2005)

That definition contains two key elements that we want to focus on:

- Directing and controlling processes.
- Assigning rights and responsibilities.

To put them in the simplest possible terms, that means how decisions are made and carried out, and who has the authority to do it – and the responsibility when they go wrong. And both of those elements are at the very heart of ESRM, and ESRM governance. ESRM is not the only model that relies on governance as a key pillar of the program. Table 7-1 offers a sample of the many standards that identify a need for strong governance for program success.

**Table 7-1. Standards and Governance Definitions**

| Standard | Commentary on Governance | Why Governance Matters in the Standard |
|---|---|---|
| **National Institute of Standards and Technology (NIST) – Framework for Improving Critical Infrastructure Cybersecurity** | "Governance (ID.GV): The policies, procedures, and processes to manage and monitor the organization's regulatory, legal, risk, environmental, and operational requirements are understood and inform the management of cybersecurity risk. | The NIST cybersecurity standard is a matrix designed to identify gaps between an existing cybersecurity program and the standards that NIST identifies as best practices for cybersecurity. |

| | ID.GV-1: Organizational information security policy is established.<br>ID.GV-2: Information security roles & responsibilities are coordinated and aligned with internal roles and external partners.<br>ID.GV-3: Legal and regulatory requirements regarding cybersecurity, including privacy and civil liberties obligations, are understood and managed.<br>ID.GV-4: Governance and risk management processes address cybersecurity risks" (National Institute of Standards and Technology, 2014, pp. 21-22). | The need for Governance is identified in the very first section of the framework, showing the importance of having the rest of the policies and processes overseen by a governing body to ensure that the policy is set, roles are assigned and supported, and risks are managed and understood.<br><br>The NIST framework, in fact, is an excellent tool to leverage in your ESRM program when identifying and assessing risks in the areas of cyber and information security. |
|---|---|---|
| **International Organization for Standardization (ISO) – ISO 31000: 2009 – Risk management – Practices and guidelines** | "Comprehensive and frequent external and internal reporting on both significant risks and on risk management performance contributes substantially to effective governance within an organization" (International Organization for Standardization, 2009, p. 23). | We have mentioned the ISO risk standard repeatedly throughout this book. The ISO standard is a comprehensive and yet easy to understand standard that should be a go-to resource for you in all aspects of running a risk-based security program.<br><br>Here we want to note that governance is so intrinsic to the ISO standard as a key piece that they don't really specifically call it out as a separate need. The need for governance is woven through the entire document as seen in the quote here. |

| OCEG GRC Capability Model (Red eBook) 2.0 | "In the context of [governance, risk, and compliance], effective corporate governance supported and in layers throughout the organization, with the emphasis in processes that affect and influence Board understanding of critical information that allows good decision-making" (Mitchell & Switzer, 2009, p. Intro-10). | The Open Compliance & Ethics Group (OCEG) is a non-profit organization dedicated to assisting global corporations with governance, risk, and compliance (GRC). Their emphasis on governance as a tool for good decision-making aligns perfectly with the ESRM methodology for working with your risk owners to determine the best treatment for security risks. Learning more about GRC through this organization can help you become better-versed in the business language of risk. |
|---|---|---|
| **ISACA COBIT 5: A Business Framework for the Governance and Management of Enterprise IT** | "Governance can be applied to the entire enterprise, an entity, a tangible or intangible asset, etc. That is, it's possible to define different views of the enterprise to which governance is applied, and it's essential to define this scope of the governance system well." (COBIT 5, 2012, p. 23). | ISACA's COBIT 5 is another framework that can be leveraged in the area of information security. It leans heavily on governance as the mechanism for standards enforcement rather than assigning that task to one specific group. Like ESRM, the COBIT model highlights the need for strong oversight to ensure that risks to the organization are being properly managed. |
| **Federation of European Risk Management Associations (FERMA) - Risk Management Standard** | Good corporate governance requires that companies adopt a methodical approach to risk management which: protects the interests of their stakeholders; ensures that the board of directors discharges its duties to direct strategy, build value, and monitor | While many of the standards we've discussed are global, European standards are often a little more strict than others, as Europe is a leading force in the area of privacy and corporate governance accountability. |

| | performance of the organization; ensures that management controls are in place and are performing adequately (Federation of European Risk Management Associations, 2002, p. 12). | Both the FERMA standard and the Solvency II directive below highlight the need for risk management to be controlled by a central governing group.

If your firm is based in Europe or has a presence there, these two standards should be at the top of your reading list when implementing your ESRM governance program. |
|---|---|---|
| **EU Solvency II Directive (2009/138/EC)** | "The system of governance includes the risk-management function, the compliance function, the internal audit function, and the actuarial function" (European Parliament and Council of the European Union, 2009, p. 4).

"Member States shall require all insurance and reinsurance undertakings to have in place an effective system of governance which provides sound and prudent management of the business. That system shall at least include an adequate transparent organizational structure with a clear allocation and appropriate segregation of responsibilities and an effective system for ensuring the transmission of information" (European Parliament and Council of the European Union, 2009, p. 33). | Unlike the voluntary FERMA standards, Solvency II, as it's called, is an actual EU council directive.

Sometimes governance is a good practice to ensure you are protecting yourself, your stakeholders, and your organization. Sometimes, as is the case here, and with Sarbanes Oxley in the US, it's the law. |

## 7.2 How Does Corporate Governance Apply to ESRM?

Corporate governance is a high-level concept that covers literally all enterprise activities. To use the term we discussed in detail in the last section, it has an extremely broad *scope*. When you're trying to understand ESRM governance, it may help to think of it as a subset of corporate governance. (It's a little like the difference between enterprise risk management (ERM) and ESRM, which was covered earlier.) Governance is governance, and governance processes are generally the same. The key difference is in the scope of what's being covered and, of course, who's responsible for it.

- In corporate governance, the controlling body is the board of directors.
- In ESRM, it's – or at least should be, in most cases – the enterprise's security council.

The security council is the body that is responsible for creating and approving the enterprise's security policy and ensuring that the security program supports the enterprise's goals. And, even more important, it's the body that has the final word on security and security risk decisions – the one that will make the tie-breaking decisions on any disagreements between stakeholders about risk mitigation or acceptance.

We'll be discussing the concept of and the need for a security council because the security council is the ESRM program's "higher authority" – and, when organized and managed effectively, the group that can do the most to help the program evolve and mature.

As the graphic in Figure 7-1 shows, the makeup, membership, and reporting structure of the security council will depend on the specific requirements of your enterprise.

The security council is responsible for the overall governance of the security program. Membership will depend on the makeup of your organization.

A security council is not *absolutely* essential for ESRM success, but we've come to believe that the creation of a security council is a clear best practice for the successful design, development, and management of an ESRM program.

*Figure 7-1. Security Council Representatives Will Vary According To Enterprise Makeup*

## 7.3 The Security Council's Role in ESRM

The security council is an example of what is known in the larger business world as a governing body. The governing body of any enterprise program is essentially a scaled-down version of the enterprise's board of directors. Just as the board has the ultimate responsibility for all aspects of overall company performance and behavior, a governing body has the responsibility for a specific program or practice. In this case, the security council is responsible for ensuring that the ESRM program is carried out as intended.

Let's take a closer look at the *OECD Principles of Corporate Governance*. The principles are intended to specifically address boards of directors, but some of them also apply to a properly implemented security council, and we've excerpted (and paraphrased slightly) a few of them here.

- Members should act on a fully informed basis, in good faith, with due diligence and care, and in the best interest of the company and the shareholders.
- Where decisions may affect different groups differently, the board should treat all fairly.
- Members should fulfil certain key functions, including:
  o Reviewing and guiding corporate strategy, major plans of action, risk policy, annual budgets, and business plans; setting objectives; monitoring implementation and performance; and overseeing major security expenditures, acquisitions and divestitures.
  o Monitoring the effectiveness of the company's practices and making changes as needed.
- If there is a potential for conflict of interest, a sufficient number of non-security members capable of exercising independent judgment to tasks should be assigned (Organisation for Economic Co-operation and Development, 2015).

Looking at this list, you can consider how the general objectives and standards of corporate governance apply to ESRM governance, as well. Here are a few sections from a real-world example: an actual charter that was put into place in a publicly traded company. The specifics of the company structure have been removed, but the charter shows how the governance structure was set up and defined to give the company's security council the responsibility and authority it needed to properly govern the ESRM program. This is a sample only, and if you choose to use this as a basis for your own program, it will need to be modified to fit the specifics of your enterprise.

### Example: A Security Council Charter – XYZ Company

#### Security Council Mission and Purpose

The XYZ Company Security Council provides leadership and direction in developing XYZ's security strategy.

The Council's mission is to facilitate communication among security risk stakeholders about XYZ's security-related policies, initiatives, and projects, and to escalate key risk decisions to senior management and the Board of Directors when appropriate.

#### Security Council Objectives

The XYZ Security Council objectives are:

- To provide overall governance to XYZ's security risk management program.
- To serve as executive sponsors of XYZ's security risk management program, providing both credibility and visibility for security-related initiatives.
- To act as a collaborative venue for groups within XYZ responsible for security risk.
- To facilitate business agreement on an acceptable risk level for XYZ.
- To facilitate prioritizing enterprise security initiatives based on business needs.
- To foster the creation and adoption of consistent and complete security policies, standards, and procedures to protect XYZ information resources.
- To review and, if necessary, respond to changes in the environment which call for corresponding changes in the XYZ risk posture.
- To continually mature XYZ's overall security strategy through identification, monitoring, and appropriate mitigation of identified security risks.
- To sponsor programs to raise awareness about security risks across XYZ.
- To initiate ad hoc security projects as needed.

## Security Council Authority

The XYZ Security Council has the authority:

- To find consensus in prioritizing security-related projects with impacted business units.
- To provide guidance around funding needs for security risk-related resources and projects.
- To review and recommend adjustments to XYZ policies or policy implementation.
- To recommend third-party assessments or independent post-incident reviews as needed.

## Security Council Roles and Responsibilities

The Security Council is composed of members of senior management from business areas responsible for monitoring and protecting against security risk. The council has primary responsibility for oversight of all aspects of security and acts as the central management and information clearinghouse for any catastrophic security-related incidents.

*All Council Members*

- Stay current on security best practices through engagement and interaction with industry experts, seminars, and other methods.
- Attend all council meetings.
- Promote discussion of concerns of their specific area of responsibility.
- Participate to define and resolve technical security problems.
- Disseminate relevant discussions and decisions to the appropriate personnel within their areas of responsibility.

- Council Chair
  - Provide overall leadership of the council.
  - Ensure that the council's work is appropriate with respect to the company's overall strategic vision.
- Council Secretary
  - Manage the logistics of the council's operation.
  - Agendas/minutes/etc.
- Enterprise Security Risk Representative
  - Ensure that the risk model(s) used by the council integrate with the company's existing risk models.
- Technology Representatives
  - Provide technical guidance and vulnerability/threat information as applicable.
  - Assist the council in converting strategic goals into tactical objectives.
  - Provide subject matter expertise as required.
- Legal Representatives
  - Ensure that proposals brought to the council adhere to company legal requirements.
  - Ensure that council actions adequately protect XYZ customer and employee privacy and security.
- Public Relations Representative
  - Coordinate security-related corporate emergency communications plans and activities.
  - Ensure communications plans exist for all core constituencies, including management, employees, government agencies, securities regulators, investors, customers, and the public.

## 7.4 Setting Up a Security Council

The process of setting up a security council begins with ensuring that the enterprise's senior decision-makers understand and accept the importance of overall governance of the ESRM program. Depending on the enterprise, this might be accomplished through a few simple conversations, or it might require a fully developed strategic planning document. Only your enterprise's executives, with guidance from you as the security and ESRM subject-matter expert – and perhaps with some assistance from this book – will know what the most appropriate approach is for your enterprise.

After you've done the basic preparations – exploring and understanding the business environment, especially its stakeholders and its assets – you should have enough knowledge to gain the support you need to define and set up the security council. That's a process that has five basic steps.

**Step 1: Define the Security Council Stakeholders**

Identify all the groups, roles, and individuals – besides the security organization – with a stake in protecting the enterprise's assets, and ensure that they all have representation on the security council. See Figure 7-2 for an example of potential council members. (The membership is likely to expand as the council is implemented).

**Step 2: Define the Mission, Objectives, and Goals of the Security Council and Document Them in a Council Charter**

See the sample charter included above for an example of how you might write a charter for your security council.

**Step 3: Define Measurements/Project Key Performance Indicators (KPIs) for ESRM**

Working with the individuals who are named as

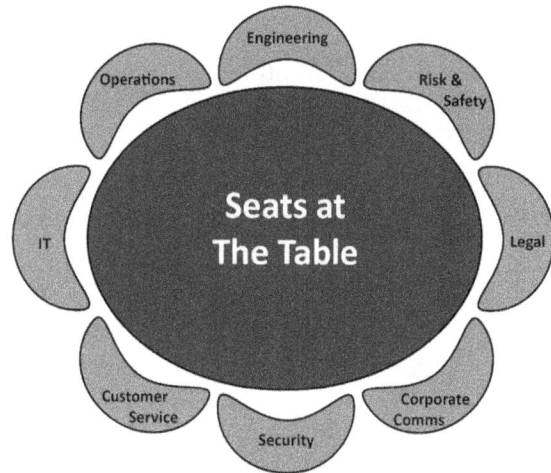

*Figure 7-2. The Security Council Represents Business Functions*

members of the security council, develop an appropriate list of measurements and KPIs to track and report to the council, in order to provide them with the information they'll need to direct the ESRM program. We'll be discussing reporting and metrics in detail later in this book.

**Step 4: Develop a List of Potential Quick "Wins" for the ESRM Program**

Develop a list of open risks that can be addressed relatively quickly (easily closed gaps, vulnerabilities that can be mitigated quickly, awareness programs, or policies that can be enacted without extended timelines) if the necessary resources and priorities are assigned to them. This will allow the newly developed council to have hard targets to focus on from the beginning of the implementation – targets that have a high likelihood of success that will give the ESRM program further credibility.

**Step 5: Begin the Process of Meeting, Reviewing, and Directing the Program According to the Council Charter**

Once a fully functioning security council is in place, your ESRM program governance is ensured.

### 7.4.1 Security's Role on the Security Council: What It Is and What It Is Not

Up to this point, we've discussed ESRM governance – and the security council's role in it – in mostly abstract terms. But what does all of that language about roles, responsibilities, charters, and authority actually mean when it comes time to practice ESRM in your company? What is it, exactly, that you're asking of your security council? And what is the dividing line between the recommendations made by the security professional and the decisions made by the governing body?

That last question is probably the most important one, because the answer to it lies in one of the foundational principles of ESRM: Risk decisions should be made by the risk owner, not by the security department.

In the case of overall ESRM governance, the security council represents the risk owner(s) and is part of that risk decision process.

### 7.4.1.1 What the Role of the Security Practitioner Is

The security leader, working in close collaboration with all strategic partners, will be responsible for setting up the security council and the governance model.

The security practitioner should also represent the security function on the council. You will advise the council on topics and risks; suggest agenda items; provide presentations; and essentially function as the security subject matter expert.

It is also appropriate to have sub-councils and security council working groups for various specific projects or programs. Those can be chaired by security to implement and execute work coming directly out of the council meetings and could be a standing working group or staffed by project.

### 7.4.1.2 What the Role of the Security Practitioner Is Not

Security should unquestionably have a place at the council table. But you shouldn't try to "run" the council or influence it beyond making recommendations for it to consider. That's why the one individual who should never be the head of the security council is the representative from the security organization.

It may be tempting to try to "stack the deck" by nominating individuals for the security council you think will agree with your recommendations. And it may also be tempting to try to shape the council's agenda by introducing only security risk issues that are important to you. There may be short-term political advantage to this security-centric approach, but the result will inevitably be a weaker security council and a weaker ESRM governance process. The council should be as *inclusive* and *independent* as possible, with members who won't just decide on the issues security raises, but will bring their own risk issues and assessments to the table. That way, once the council is in place, and all the members clearly understand their roles, you can be certain that it's looking at what's important, not just to you as the security representative but to the entire enterprise.

The security council, as we've already mentioned, is the enterprise's security risk governing body – and you shouldn't try to govern the governing. In fact, as paradoxical as it may sound, the best way to lead is to follow. Once you've set up the council and established its rules and procedures, you need to follow them, even when you don't agree with the decisions the council makes. That will inevitably be frustrating at times, but if you remember your ESRM principles, there should also be satisfaction in knowing that even if the council isn't doing exactly what you think it should be, it's doing it according to the practices and processes you defined.

# 8

# Where Should Security Report in an Organization Structure?

It's always been challenging to determine where in the enterprise the security organization should report. While your security council is the strategic governing body of the ESRM program and plays an important role in ensuring that it has high-level executive input and commitment, as well as authority and independence, the security council is not a day-to-day managing function. So in addition to the strategic guidance of the council, it's important to have an operational reporting structure for the security organization that makes it possible to carry out the tactical functions of the ESRM program.

## 8.1 Reporting Options

Here are a few of the reporting arrangements we have heard of in discussions with our peers in the security profession:

- The security organization could report to HR because the security organization – especially in its physical security activities – protects the enterprise's employees.
- It could roll up under operations because protecting the enterprise's operational capabilities – its business – is its primary purpose.
- The finance organization is another possibility because it has a significant interest in mitigating enterprise risk already.

These reporting arrangements are all commonplace – too commonplace, in our view. It's easy to understand why some enterprises choose to structure their security organizations this way, but reporting into HR, operations, finance, or any other comparatively narrow-scope organization almost always delivers less than optimal results. These reporting lines are not optimal because they don't allow for full transparency, independence, or proper authority. Oftentimes they even carry inherent conflicts of interest. Additionally, these organizations do not have enterprise-wide responsibility for corporate governance or regulatory compliance.

A main reason that businesses struggle with where to align security in an organization, and how it ends up in many of the reporting structures listed above, is because we as an industry have not clearly defined the security role and hence organization leaders, as we discussed earlier, see the security function defined by the tasks it has been assigned.

We recommend that, for most enterprises, the security department should report to a function within the organization that provides clear independence, has proper authority, and can easily make security risks transparent. It is also important that using that criteria, security reside at the highest possible level in the organization to allow for proper scope for security risk management.

> ➤ Security should report directly to the general counsel, the CEO, or even the board of directors – all of which have corporate governance and regulatory compliance responsibilities of which security is a key part.

## 8.2 What Does Security Need to Be Successful?

In order to determine the best structure for your security organization and your enterprise, the first question you and the enterprise's executives need to ask is: ***What does security need in my enterprise to be successful?***

The simple, immediate answer is, security needs independence and proper authority – independence so that it can properly identify risks across the enterprise, and authority to make those risks transparent. But applying that simple answer in the real world isn't always quite so simple. One reason for having a security council in place as a strategic governing body is that it makes it possible for many different security and risk stakeholders to have a say in very important questions like this one.

## 8.3 Some Lines of Reporting Carry Obvious Conflicts

Operational lines of reporting carry with them obvious conflicts. (We discussed some of them earlier.) A security organization reporting into an operational function – the chief operating officer (COO), or the IT, sales, or finance organizations – will likely struggle to maintain independence and transparency. It's not difficult to understand why.

Here are just a few examples of potential conflicts:

- If security reports into the finance organization, will it be comfortable investigating the possibility of fraud or other financial misconduct?
- If it reports to the CIO, will it be comfortable reporting on security risks that reflect poorly on the IT organization?
- If it reports to the COO, will it be comfortable recommending risk mitigation methods that might slow down important business operations?

We think the answer to all those questions is clearly "No."

## 8.4 Greatest Success Comes with the Greatest Independence

We've come to the conclusion based on our own experience and discussions with many other security professionals over the years that the best practice is to have the security department report into functions or organizations that also require independence.

These include the legal/compliance and internal audit organizations, and the board of directors. Obviously, the CEO's office, because of its authority and legal responsibility to expose risk, also makes for a high-quality reporting line. Any of these more independent internal organizations would be a good place for the security organization, and the ESRM program, to function in.

The key for your program is to ensure that the ultimate reporting line is to a leader who understands the importance of and has the authority to ensure independence, authority, and appropriate scope. Once again, these questions of strategy and direction can be driven by the security council, if an appropriate

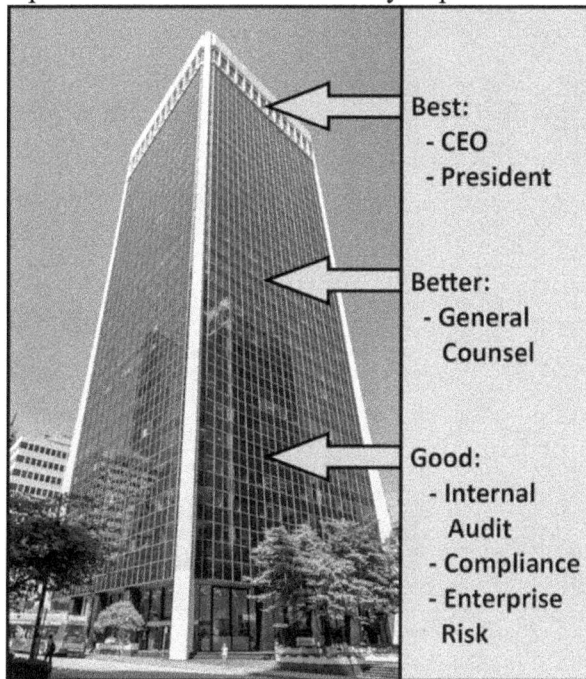

*Figure 8-1. The Higher the Security Reporting Structure, the More Effective It Will Be*

reporting structure can't be developed. In the picture here, we show a sampling of potential reporting relationships. As you can see in Figure 8-1, the higher in the enterprise your security organization reports, the more successful it's likely to be.

# 9

# What Do Executives Need to Know About ESRM?

In writing this book, one of our hopes is to save you some time in determining the best course of action in rolling out an ESRM program. Therefore, in this section, we will focus on some ways to explain ESRM in business terms that your executives can relate to, and some tactics for showing them the value of an ESRM program. Throughout this book, we've discussed the benefits of ESRM, the success implementing a risk-based security approach can bring to you as a professional and your program overall, and the value it can bring to your enterprise. But we also mentioned that it's critical to have executive understanding of the ESRM concept overall and buy-in and support of you implementing the approach in your organization.

## 9.1 The Challenge of Executive Support

In rolling out your ESRM program, one of the most critical aspects of moving into an ESRM paradigm is obtaining executive buy-in and support. That can sometimes be a lengthy and daunting process. We understand that – we have had these executive level conversations many times now, with different executives in different enterprises. We will share some of the keys to having these conversations. First, though, a story of the first time we undertook the process of convincing executives in our organization of the value of ESRM.

### Case study: Communicating ESRM to Executives

From the beginning of our ESRM program rollout, it was clear that we would need executive support and understanding to accomplish our goals. We started the process of getting that executive support by speaking with the chief executive officer (CEO) and the general counsel, both roles that require an innate understanding of risk and risk management. First, we explained how we understood the security role, in ESRM terms, and asked them whether they agreed with our view. Now, agreement didn't come overnight. These were tough-minded people who were perfectly comfortable saying no if they thought that was the right answer. They asked us hard questions about ESRM, about what managing security risk meant, about how the process worked. We actually had to go back a few times – to refine our answers, dig deeper into how we were presenting risk-based security, and explain why it was best for the enterprise. But they finally came to agree with our view of security's role as managers of security risk in partnership with the business. Still, we didn't stop there. We kept reminding the CEO in particular at the beginning of any subsequent meeting, "This is how we see our role. Do you still agree?" This was about making sure there was a clear and accepted understanding of our role before we discussed other security business, because those further discussions had to be based on our strategic partners' buy-in. Getting executive buy-in as we did then firmly established the *scope* of responsibility and *authority* of the program, allowing us to implement our ESRM program with *independence* and *transparency.* Once we had agreement at the highest levels in the company, we were able to go to other department leaders and explain to them what ESRM was, and what it meant for us and – crucially – for them and their success in protecting their assets.

Please understand, although we devoted only a paragraph to describing the process, this change in viewpoint and buy-in of our role didn't happen overnight with our strategic partners. One thing that always made us laugh (and was a consistent reminder of how much more work we had in front of us to bring more understanding of the role of security as managers of risk) was that even after we had the support of our executives, we would be invited to the senior leadership strategy meetings and someone at the meeting would inevitably come up and say, "Are we safe here?" or "Watching over the boss, huh?" Now, we may have had an affirmative answer for both, but the point was that we were there to understand the direction of the company and help the business strategize to protect the company in it's efforts to be successful. Clearly,we still needed to get to everyone in that room and advance the understanding of what our role was, and eventually we did.

## 9.2 Communicating ESRM Concepts to the Executive

Your executives, in order to properly understand and support risk-based security, must first come to agreement with you on the need for ESRM and with the premise behind the philosophy on the role of security in the enterprise. When discussing ESRM with senior executives, there are a few main points that are critical to communicate about the philosophy and program. We recommend focusing on just a few points, as the opportunity to speak at length or in depth may not always be available.

### 9.2.1 For the Executive: Understand the Underlying Philosophy of ESRM and the Role of Security

The main things your enterprise executives need to understand about ESRM are listed in Table 9-1.

**Table 9-1. The Partnership Between Security and Other Enterprise Business Functions**

| The Role of Security | The Role of Business Function Leaders |
|---|---|
| Manage security risks to enterprise assets. | Understand the role of the security department in helping the business carry out its operational mission. |
| Monitor risks to ensure impacts stay within defined tolerance levels. | Define an acceptable level of security risk tolerance to assets in their area of responsibility. |
| Provide subject matter expertise on risk mitigation options. | Make quality, educated decisions on security risks to assets in their area of responsibility. |

| Carry out risk mitigation tasks that require technical security skills in support of the security/business partnership. | Carry out risk mitigation tasks that require business function involvement in support of the security/business partnership. |
|---|---|

To narrow it to an even more concise message, you might say:

- The role of security is to manage security risk.
- This means the security team provides security guidance and subject matter expertise to business function leaders to help them make quality security risk decisions in their areas of responsibility.

When presenting to your executives, you can tailor your message to include as much or as little information on risk-based security management. As with much of what we have discussed in this book, you'll need to conform to what you've learned about your enterprise and leadership throughout the course of understanding your enterprise in order to effectively have this conversation.

However, it is absolutely critical that you are able to get executive buy-in and support for the ESRM program. Without that executive support, you will have trouble getting the needed independence, transparency, authority, and scope that you need for your program.

One way to explain to your enterprise executives why a security program needs their support is to explain it through the lens of other risk-based programs.

### 9.2.2 For the Executive: Understand ESRM Parallels with Other Risk-Based Functions

Change can be difficult, especially in large enterprises where making fundamental shifts in philosophy requires time and can impact significant populations. In all instances, communicating the need for change must be clear and factual. Oftentimes, even perfectly reasonable requests for independence, transparency, authority, or scope can be perceived from the outside as "kingdom-building" or a "land grab." But with ESRM, the security role is only concerned with protecting the business in the ways that business organization deems appropriate. Therefore, drawing parallels with other areas that have the same protective function and goal as you explain the need for these four elements can be an effective persuasion tool.

Security, when practiced following ESRM principles, shares many traits with audit, compliance, legal, and other risk management functions. Nobody would expect an auditing team to do an effective job if the organization being audited was not open and honest, or if the target of the audit was in a position of authority over the audit team. The reverse is also true – the auditors must be equally open and honest about what they are doing, and have the authority and scope to do it. By understanding what audit teams and compliance teams do, and what *their* success factors are, you can learn how to promote transparency, independence, authority, and scope in your ESRM program.

### 9.2.2.1 For the Security Practitioner: What Are Audit, Legal, and Compliance?

To start, let's look at the definitions that some audit, legal, and compliance organizations use to describe themselves:

#### *Audit*

From the Institute of Internal Auditors (IIA):

> "Internal auditing is an independent, objective assurance and consulting activity designed to add value and improve an organization's operations. It helps an organization accomplish its objectives by bringing a systematic, disciplined approach to evaluate and improve the effectiveness of risk management, control, and governance processes." (n.d., p. 3)

From the Association of Certified Fraud Examiners website:

> "Internal auditors verify internal controls are in place and functioning properly to deter fraud. Internal auditors conduct compliance and operational audits, offering solutions for weaknesses in internal controls and verifying that all laws and regulations are upheld."

#### *Legal (General or Corporate Counsel)*

From the Society for Human Resources Management (SHRM) job description site, pertaining to the role of the general counsel:

> "The general counsel is responsible for leading corporate strategic and tactical legal initiatives. The general counsel provides senior management with effective advice on company strategies and their implementation, manages the legal function, and obtains and oversees the work of outside counsel. The general counsel is directly involved in complex business transactions in negotiating critical contracts."

#### *Ethics and Compliance*

From the US Sentencing Commission 2012 *Guidelines Manual*:

> "[A] compliance and ethics program shall be reasonably designed, implemented, and enforced so that the program is generally effective in preventing and detecting criminal conduct... An organization's program should include monitoring and auditing systems that are designed to detect criminal and other improper conduct." (§ 8B2.1)

Compliance officers and auditors under them are charged by law with implementing and carrying out these programs.

### 9.2.2.2 For the Security Practitioner: What Do Audit, Legal, and Compliance Functions Need for Success?

The foundational requirements for success in audit, legal, and compliance are remarkably similar to the ESRM success factors we discussed above. Even if they don't use exactly the same words, you'll see independence, transparency, authority, and scope are constant themes in the compliance and audit professions.

Donna Boehme, with the industry group Compliance Strategists, wrote in *Compliance Today* (2012) about the essential features of the chief ethics and compliance officer (CECO) position, singling out some that mirror our discussion here.

> "Line of sight – The Chief Ethics and Compliance Officer (CECO) must have unfettered access to relevant information to be able to form independent opinions and manage the program effectively. Where important areas of risk … are 'carved out' from the CECO's line of sight, the CECO will be unable to perform adequate oversight of the program for that risk...." (p. 24).

Doesn't that sound like what we've been calling *risk transparency*: the ability to see and have access to what you need?

> "Empowerment – The CECO must have the appropriate unambiguous mandate, delegation of authority, senior-level positioning, and empowerment to carry out his/her duties" (p. 23).

The word Boehme uses is *empowerment*, but it's what we discussed above in needing the authority to carry out your defined role.

> "Independence – The CECO must have sufficient authority and independence to oversee the integrity of the compliance program" (p.23).

Here we even have the same terminology, and that's not surprising, because we're not alone in saying a risk-based function – any risk-based function – needs these essential foundations. We're simply expanding the sphere of risk-based functions to include security.

The IIA (2016) calls out several similar points on its web page detailing the *Core Principles for the Professional Practice of Internal Auditing*, stating that "for an internal audit function to be considered effective, all Principles should be present and operating effectively." And – no surprise here – in the IIA's list of core principles, we find parallels with independence, scope, and authority:

- "Is objective and free from undue influence (independent).
- Aligns with the strategies, objectives, and risks of the organization.
- Is appropriately positioned and adequately resourced."

In the area of the legal department and general counsel, we see similar themes. From an article reprinted on the Ethic-Intelligence website by Daniel Lucien Bühr and Herbert Wohlmann:

"The General Counsel has a dual role: She/he is a business partner who assists management in achieving the operational goals of the company. At the same time, the General Counsel is a guardian to the company. If a conflict between both roles arises, the interests of the company must prevail. The guardian role of the General Counsel is an important element of the checks and balances of a company. The General Counsel can only be a guardian to the company, if she/he is independent. The key elements of organizational independence of the General Counsel are a direct (solid) reporting line to the CEO and a (dotted) strategic reporting line to the board." (2013, July)

We could offer many more examples of risk-based enterprise functions that have foundational concepts and principles in common with ESRM, but we think you get the idea. These are all functions that address business-critical issues of risk, and they all need the same kind of enterprise commitment and support.

## 9.3 For the Executive: What is Your Role in Supporting an ESRM Security Structure?

Essentially, the executive level of any enterprise is responsible for ensuring that the business meets the mission and objective that is laid out for it by the board of directors (or other owners in a non-board-directed organization). The top leaders are there to lead strategically, and it's their role to ensure that all of the other people in the organization have what they need to perform their role in meeting those strategic objectives.

So – what is the role of the executive leadership in regards to ESRM? Once they have agreed to the role of the security team as managers of security risk, they have one simple task: ensuring that the security group is set up for success in the enterprise. Ensuring that success means a few things.

### 9.3.1 Ensuring a Definition of Security Success

Your security program simply cannot be a success if the enterprise does not agree on the definition of a successful security program. Success must be defined by the business, by what the business wants to protect, and how they are willing to protect it. Some questions that must be answered in order to have a common definition of success for the ESRM program are:

- What is the security risk tolerance for the enterprise overall?
- Are there areas with higher or lower tolerance for security risk?
- What is the measurement of tolerance discrepancy?
- What is the methodology by which the security team will be judged as fulfilling the mission of managing security risk?
- How will the performance of security tasks that mitigate risk for the business be included in the definition of security success?

Answers to these questions will give security leadership the ability to fulfill their role of managing security risk and performing risk mitigation activities as deemed appropriate by the business.

### 9.3.2 Ensuring the Correct Security Skill Sets

Once executives have defined the criteria of success for the security program, they need to ensure that the security team has the correct skill sets for carrying out both the risk management strategic function and the risk mitigation tactical function.

Setting the security team up for success means first ensuring the security leader has the right skills to manage the ESRM program. Some questions for your executives to ask about potential security leaders are:

- Does the security leader have an understanding of business concepts like business communications, personnel leadership, finance and budgeting, and reporting?
- Does the security leader have an ability to interface with business professionals, functional leaders, business executives, and board members?
- Does the security leader have an appropriate understanding of technical security topics that fall into the scope of risk mitigation tactics?
- Does the security leader have the experience needed to lead a risk-based, not task-based, security function?
- Do the members of the security team understand risk management topics?
- Do the members of the security team have the needed security technical expertise to mitigate security risks to the business?
- Do the members of the security team embrace the ESRM philosophy?

If the security team is lacking in critical skills for protecting the enterprise from security risk in a manner consistent with the security role, it's imperative that the executive either provide training and education to close the skills gaps quickly, or find alternate or additional resources for the security team.

### 9.3.3 Ensuring the Essentials for Success Are in Place

We have mentioned repeatedly in the last few sections the absolute need for having some essential elements in order to succeed in the security program:

- Transparency.
- Independence.
- Authority.
- Scope.

The role of your enterprise executives in an ESRM program is to provide support to the security leaders and team in cases where other business function leaders question or push back on the independence, authority, transparency, or scope of the security group.

These essential traits for the security team can be controversial when first rolled out. It's possible that the security team might be seen as overstepping their boundaries if the enterprise is accustomed to seeing the role of security as managing tasks such as badges, cameras, and passwords. ESRM is a different philosophy and mindset. Executive support is critical in ensuring the entire enterprise understands the role of security and how they will be partnering with the business leaders to help them protect the assets in their area of responsibility.

Additionally, your executives must ensure that you, as the security leader, have access to the other business leaders and are meeting with them on a regular basis to ensure proper management of enterprise security risk.

### 9.3.4 Ensuring the Correct Reporting Structure

One of the most influential aspects of the security program, the thing that will essentially ensure the essential elements listed above, is the organizational reporting structure of the security department. Independence of reporting lines is, as we have outlined already, unquestionably crucial to the success of the security organization. The role of the executive in ESRM is to ensure that independence by placing the security organization in the area of the company that will provide the clearest lines of independence and authority for the program.

Depending on the enterprise, there might be several options that could provide this. A larger organization might have options such as:

- Compliance.
- Enterprise risk management.
- Internal audit.

All of these could be options for reporting. Smaller organizations might not have all of those areas, in which case, the executive's job is to find the most appropriate reporting line.

We recommend, of course, that the security department should report into senior management directly. And, depending on the nature and impact of risk to the enterprise, even have a C-level leader, reporting directly to the CEO – Chief Security Officer (CSO). If that is not possible, a CSO reporting into the general counsel is also a good option.

### 9.3.5 Ensuring the Board or Enterprise Ownership is Aware of the Role of Security and Security Risks as a Business-Critical Topic

Just as it's critical that the executive level make sure other functions inside the enterprise are aware of the role of security in helping the business protect itself from harm from security risks, it's also incumbent upon the executive leadership to make the board of directors aware of the topic of security risk. Some topics that the board should be aware of are:

- Significant security risks to the enterprise critical functions.
- Changes in major risk categories due to environmental change or changes in business products, program, mission or goals.
- Material and significant security incidents that violated tolerance levels as set by the board or executives.

## 9.4 For the Executive: What Should You Expect from the ESRM Program?

For the executives and members of the board of directors, there are some things that the security team and leadership should be providing on a regular basis. The ESRM program allows the security team to assist the enterprise in protecting itself, but the enterprise leadership must have a constant awareness of how the security organization is doing that, and what the current level of security risk to the enterprise is. Things the executive should expect to receive from the security leader are:

- Regular reporting on current and future security risks that are material to business success.
- Regular reporting on the efficient use of enterprise resources in mitigating security risk.
- Regular reporting on the security risk landscape inside and outside of the organization.
- Regular reviews of the business functions that security has met with and partnered with in managing enterprise risk.
- Escalation of security issues that exceed the tolerance levels set by executives and both the functional and top levels of the enterprise.

Many of these items should be delivered to executives on a regular basis as part of regular reporting and metrics. Security can build quality reports that assist the business in understanding the current risk picture and envisioning potential future risks that are on the strategic horizon.

# 10

# Reports and Metrics

We've discussed above the need for reporting a number of different topics on a regular basis to the executive level. Reporting metrics is one path that allows you to communicate the level of success you are having as a security program.

Reporting metrics in ESRM is very different than reporting metrics in a more traditional security environment. If you're used to operating in a task-based security environment, some reports that you might have created in the past could include:

- Security guard hours and performance.
- Security incident numbers by type or location.
- Access credential processing.
- Loss/shrinkage numbers.

In ESRM, the types of reports that you will most often provide would be:

- Incident levels that indicate security risk tolerance exceptions.
- New or residual risks identified since the last report period.
- Metrics of mitigation activities as related to risk categories.

When we look at reporting and metrics in an ESRM environment, we separate the reports into two categories. The first measures how the security risks that have been identified as important to the enterprise are faring in relation to the set tolerance level; the second reports metrics of task management, and efficiency of resource use in the department. Both are important, and they both have different sets of audiences and different information covered.

## 10.1 Metrics of Risk Tolerance

In a traditional security department, the kinds of reports that are sent to management tend to focus on how robust the department is: how much work they are doing, how many types of responses they have done, and how many hours were spent on security tasks. These efficiency reports have their place in ESRM as well, but they are not the main focus of metrics and reporting.

ESRM places a much larger focus on reports that directly communicate to the business function leaders how the mitigation plans that are in place are working to ensure that risks to the enterprise assets are remaining within the defined boundaries of tolerance. This is not a method of reporting that many security professionals are accustomed to doing, and will be a shift in how you think about and develop reports.

How can you communicate metrics of risk tolerance? First, you'll need to ask yourself some questions and think about them from the point of view of your strategic partners who will be receiving the reports.

- Who is the audience for this report?
  - You'll likely need to create separate reports for each line of business, due to disparate risks.
- What are the risks that the audience is most concerned with?
  - One general report on all risks will likely include too much information, much of it not relevant to all functions.
- What metrics will indicate to the audience whether the risk mitigation tasks are keeping the risk within tolerance levels?
  - Is a certain type of incident happening with higher frequency than the risk owner finds acceptable, even with mitigation activities happening?
- What metrics will indicate that a previously acceptable risk might be rising to exceed set tolerances?
  - Are security responses or investigations rising in a previously unmitigated risk area?

### 10.1.1 Example of a Security Report

### 10.1.1.1 Planning the Report

Now, taking each of the questions as outlined above, we'll walk through one example of building a security metrics report for the HR risk stakeholder.

- Who is the audience for this report?
  - HR – owners of risks that would most likely impact employee populations.
- What are the risks that the audience is most concerned with?
  - In this example, we will assume that your HR strategic partner has indicated a high level of interest in protecting employees against the risks of workplace violence, bullying, and harassment.
- What metrics will indicate to the audience whether the risk mitigation tasks are keeping the risk within tolerance levels?
  - Reported incidents of harassment or bullying.
  - Reported incidents of angry customers in company locations.
  - Reported incidents of assaults or vehicle break-ins on company parking lots (to name a few examples).
- What metrics will indicate that a previously acceptable risk might be rising to exceed set tolerances?

- o Reported incidents of unknown persons entering company locations might indicate instances of persons with bad intent entering facilities – this could represent issues of domestic violence spilling over into the workplace.
- o Opinions and attitudes of both security personnel and stakeholders can also change tolerance. An incident completely external to the enterprise, such as a terror attack on a similar firm in another country, might change the tolerance level of risk on some physical security risks by making people more aware of the risk itself. External events could be a reportable metric.

### 10.1.1.2 Building the Report

Once the above questions have been answered, you can put together a report for your HR strategic partner to receive. We recommend a structure that includes a past/present/future focus.

**Past:**

Trends from time period just ended (quarter or month).

- Current trends being seen around the trackable risks for that function.
- Metrics/charts/graphs in support of those trends.

**Present:**

Environmental trends that might impact risk in the next reporting period.

- Projected increases or cuts that could impact mitigation activities.
- Business changes that could impact risk.

**Future:**

Long term trends or activities to watch.

- Emerging risk trends.
- Future mitigation activities and projects planned.

This is just one example of how you might present the information. See Figure 10-1 for a possible layout you could choose.

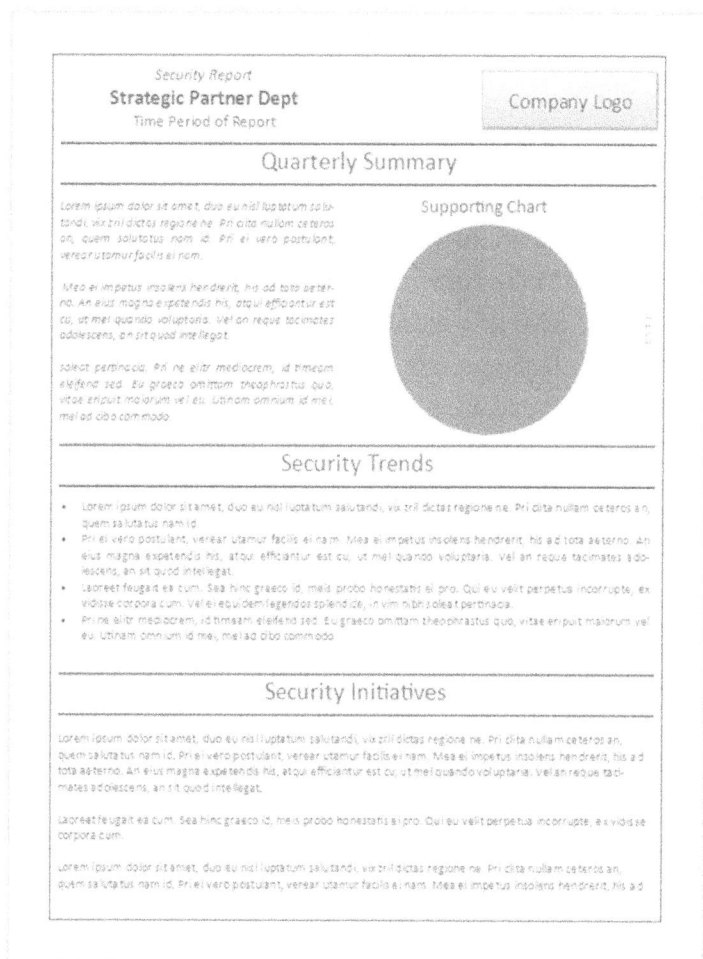

*Figure 10-1. Layout of Sample Security Report*

## 10.2 Metrics of Security Department Efficiency

Although reporting in the ESRM model is mainly focused on metrics of risk tolerance and variance, there are still instances where metrics of efficiency are important. As a department that manages risk on behalf of the business, security is a steward of budgeted funding in support of enterprise operations. It's important to be able to show that we are being responsible stewards of the funds assigned to risk mitigation activities, and metrics of efficiency are excellent reports for the direct security management structure, for finance, and for functions which directly fund security activities in support of their assets and areas of responsibility.

For those audiences with an interest in the metrics of efficiency, this is the place for you to create and disseminate the traditional security metrics around topics such as:

- Incident response.
- Investigations.
- Business support.

## 10.3 Communicating to an Executive Audience

When you're creating reports to communicate the work of the security department and the status of risk as managed by your department, you'll want to remember a few key aspects of crafting communications for the executive level.

- Make sure your data tells a story (has a reason for being in the report).
- Use graphics to present numeric information.
- Keep reports short and to the point.
- Present the data regularly.
- Use only up-to-date information in reports.
- Have appendices and backup details ready for executives who request further information.

Reporting to your business partners, management, executives, and even the board of directors is an important part of the responsibility of the security leader in an ESRM program. Communicating the value of the security function is one reason for this reporting, but in ESRM, the most important reason for communicating the reports and metrics from your group is to ensure ongoing awareness of the status of security risks in the enterprise environment.

## 10.4 A Look into the Future – A Successful ESRM Program

From both a management perspective and an individual standpoint, ESRM success will come from implementing ESRM principles consistently, throughout the security organization and in the individual security practitioner's role. Applying ESRM principles in daily roles and decision-making will lead to proactive thinking and problem-solving in dealing with security risks – and that leads to professional and personal success. So what does success look like when you're managing security risks using ESRM principles? Many of the indicators of success are intangible, and specific to your industry and role; however, here are some of the intangible benefits of ESRM, and some ideas about what ESRM success can look and feel like.

- **Knowledge and Professionalism.** Being proactive and having a firm understanding of the security role will lead to you developing a reputation for knowledge and professionalism, not only for you, but also for your organization. When you're recognized among your peers as a professional, you'll be more satisfied and more open to opportunities for growth in the security discipline as a whole, not just in a particular function.

- **Inclusion.** Here's another indicator of success: The consistent practice of ESRM will lead to your strategic partners in the organization including you, early and often, in discussions about how you can help them manage the security risks they face. That's a big difference from having them see you and your organization as a barrier to their own efficiency, slowing down their business processes. When you're managing with ESRM principles, you'll be guiding your stakeholders through the collaborative process of identifying risks to their assets and developing mitigation plans for them. You'll be a true partner to the business function leaders, and you'll find you're included in the business process more and more.

- **Satisfaction.** Last, but definitely not least, there's job satisfaction. When you manage security risks with ESRM, your job will become much more satisfying and much less frustrating. You'll truly understand the security role, know how to practice security professionally, and be better-positioned to make – and defend – security risk recommendations.

Security is a blend of art and science. Balancing the two requires judgment and discretion, putting in the right amount of effort to protect an asset – someone else's asset, with someone else's defined value. It isn't easy, but when you get the balance right, the result will be a successful ESRM program, and a successful career as a security practitioner.

# References

The Association of Certified Fraud Examiners (ACFE). (2016). *Internal auditor.* Retrieved from
http://www.acfe.com/internal-auditor.aspx

Bernard, R. (2011, April). *The state of converged security operations.* Retrieved from
http://www.securityinfowatch.com/article/10247031/the-state-of-converged-security-operations

Boehme, D. (2012, December). Five essential features of the chief ethics and compliance officer
position. *Compliance Today* (pp. 22-25). Retrieved from http://www.hcca-info.org/Portals/0/PDFs/Resources/Compliance_Today/1212/CT_1212_Boehme.pdf

Bourne, L. (2005). *Project relationship management and the stakeholder circle* (Doctoral
dissertation). Retrieved from http://www.stakeholder-management.com/Papers/P021_L_Bourne_Thesis.pdf

Bourne, L. (2008, May). *SRMM: Stakeholder relationship management maturity.* Retrieved from
http://www.stakeholdermapping.com/index.php/download_file/view/30/92/

Bühr, D. L., & Wohlmann, H. (2013, July). Top five governance principles for the corporate
legal function. *Ethic-Intelligence.* Retrieved from http://www.ethic-intelligence.com/experts/318-is-there-a-need-for-good-governance-in-the-corporate-legal-function/

*COBIT 5: A business framework for the governance and management of enterprise IT.* (2012).
Rolling Meadows, IL: ISACA.

Committee of Sponsoring Organizations of the Treadway Commission (COSO). (2004,
September). *Enterprise risk management – Integrated framework.* Durham, NC:
American Institute of Certified Public Accountants.

The CSO Roundtable of ASIS International. (2010, April). *Enterprise security risk management:
How great risks lead to great deeds* [White paper]. Retrieved from
https://cso.asisonline.org/esrm/Documents/CSORT_ESRM_whitepaper_%20pt%201.pdf

The CSO Roundtable of ASIS International. (2015, January). *Enterprise security risk management: A holistic approach to security* [White paper]. (Access requires registration with ASIS.)

Dowdney, A. (2005, December 1). Corporate governance in the UK and U.S. comparison. *Metropolitan Corporate Council*. Retrieved from http://www.metrocorpcounsel.com/articles/6173/corporate-governance-uk-and-us-comparison

European Parliament and Council of the European Union. (2009, December). Directive 2009/138/EC on the taking up and pursuit of insurance and reinsurance. *Official Journal of the European Union*, L 335. Retrieved from http://www.tsb.org.tr/images/Documents/SolvencyIIDirektifi.pdf

Federation of European Risk Management Associations (FERMA). (2002). *A risk management standard.* Brussels, Belgium: Author.

Institute of Internal Auditors (IIA). (2016). *Core principles for the professional practice of internal auditing.* Retrieved from https://na.theiia.org/standards-guidance/mandatory-guidance/Pages/Core-Principles-for-the-Professional-Practice-of-Internal-Auditing.aspx

Institute of Internal Auditors (IIA). (n.d.). *The framework for internal audit effectiveness: The new IPPF* (p. 3). Retrieved from https://na.theiia.org/standards-guidance/Public%20Documents/The-Framework-for-Internal-Audit-Effectiveness-The-New-IPPF-Brochure.pdf

International Organization for Standardization (ISO). (2009). *ISO/IEC 31000:2009 Risk management – Principles and guidelines.* Geneva, Switzerland: Author.

Kelley, D., & Kelley, T. (2012, December). Reclaim your creative confidence. *Harvard Business Review.* Retrieved from https://hbr.org/2012/12/reclaim-your-creative-confidence

Mitchell, S. L., & Switzer, C. S. (2009, April). *GRC capability model "red book" 2.0.* Scottsdale, AZ: Open Compliance & Ethics Group.

National Institute of Standards and Technology (NIST). (2012*). Guide for conducting risk assessments* [NIST Special Publication 800 - 30]. Gaithersburg, MD: Author.

National Institute of Standards and Technology (NIST). (2014, February*). Framework for improving critical infrastructure cybersecurity.* Gaithersburg, MD: Author.

Needle, D. (2010). *Business in context: An introduction to business and its environment.* Andover, Hampshire, UK: Cengage Learning EMEA.

The Organisation for Economic Co-operation and Development (OECD). (2005, July). Corporate governance. In *Glossary of statistical terms*. Retrieved from https://stats.oecd.org/glossary/detail.asp?ID=6778

The Organisation for Economic Co-operation and Development (OECD). (2015). *G20/OECD Principles of Corporate Governance*. Paris, France: Author.

PricewaterhouseCoopers. (2008). *A practical guide to risk assessment: How principles-based risk assessment enables organizations to take the right risks* [White paper]. Retrieved from https://web.actuaries.ie/sites/default/files/erm-resources/A%20practical%20guide%20to%20risk%20assessment.pdf

Prince, B. (2015, February). Target data breach tally hits $162 million in net costs. *Security Week*. Retrieved from http://www.securityweek.com/target-data-breach-tally-hits-162-million-net-costs

Society for Human Resources Management. (n.d.). *Job descriptions: General counsel*. (Membership required for access.)

Stanford University Institute of Design. (2013). *Bootcamp bootleg*. Retrieved from http://dschool.stanford.edu/wp-content/uploads/2013/10/METHODCARDS-v3-slim.pdf

US Sentencing Commission. (2012). *Guidelines Manual* (§ 8B2.1.). Retrieved from http://www.ussc.gov/guidelines-manual/2012/2012-8b21

# Credits

**Kristen Noakes-Fry, ABCI**, is Executive Editor at Rothstein Publishing. Previously, she was a Research Director, Information Security and Risk Group, for Gartner, Inc.; Associate Editor at Datapro (McGraw-Hill), where she was responsible for *Datapro Reports on Information Security*; and Associate Professor of English at Atlantic Cape College in New Jersey. She holds an M.A. from New York University and a B.A. from Russell Sage College.

| | |
|---|---|
| **Cover Design and Graphics:** | Sheila Kwiatek, Flower Grafix |
| **eBook Design & Processing:** | Donna Luther, Metadata Prime |
| **Copy Editing:** | Nancy M. Warner |
| **Publishing & Marketing Intern:** | Sarah Patton |

ROTHSTEIN PUBLISHING
A Division of Rothstein Associates Inc.

**Philip Jan Rothstein, FBCI**, is President of Rothstein Associates Inc., a management consultancy he founded in 1984 as a pioneer in the disciplines of Business Continuity and Disaster Recovery. He is also the Executive Publisher of Rothstein Publishing.

**Rothstein Publishing** is your premier source of books and learning materials about Business Resilience, including Crisis Management, Business Continuity, Disaster Recovery, Emergency Management, Security, and Risk Management. Our industry-leading authors provide current, actionable knowledge, solutions, and tools you can put in practice immediately. Rothstein Publishing remains true to the decades-long commitment of Rothstein Associates, which is to prepare you and your organization to protect, preserve, and recover what is most important: your people, facilities, assets, and reputation.

# About the Authors

**Brian Allen** has more than 20 years' experience in virtually every aspect of the security field. He most recently held the position of Chief Security Officer (CSO) with Time Warner Cable (TWC), a leading multinational provider of telecommunications, information, and entertainment services headquartered in New York City. In this role, he was responsible for protecting TWC's assets worldwide, coordinating the company's crisis management and business continuity management (BCM) programs, managing TWC's cybersecurity policy and leading its security risk management program. He managed the company's security policy and relations with law enforcement and government authorities, as well as all customer security risk issues, oversaw internal and external investigations, and headed the company's workplace violence program. Before joining TWC in January 2002, he was Director of the Office of Cable Signal Theft at the National Cable and Telecommunications Association in Washington, D.C., and the owner of ACI Investigations, a multimillion-dollar provider of security guard, investigations, and consulting services.

Brian earned his Bachelor of Science degree in criminal justice from Long Island University and received his Juris Doctor degree from Touro Law Center in New York. He is a member of the New York State Bar Association, a Certified Protection Professional (CPP) with ASIS, a Certified Information Systems Security Professional (CISSP) with ISC2, a Certified Fraud Examiner (CFE) with the ACFE and a Certified Information Security Manager (CISM) with ISACA. Brian is also a member of the International Security Management Association and the Association of Threat Assessment Professionals.

Brian is an Adjunct Professor at the University of Connecticut, School of Business MBA Program and is active in industry organizations. He served as a member of the Communications

Infrastructure Reliability and Interoperability Council (CSRIC), an FCC appointed position, and co-chaired its working group on Cybersecurity Best Practices and the Cybersecurity Framework. He is also one of four elected communications company representatives to serve on the Executive Committee of the US Communications Sector Coordinating Council (CSCC). He works with the Cross Sector Cybersecurity Working Group, established by the U.S. Department of Homeland Security (DHS) under the Critical Infrastructure Partnership Advisory Council. Brian has served on the board of directors of ASIS International, and the board of trustees of ASIS International's Foundation. He is currently a member of the Board of Directors of the Domestic Violence Crisis Center in Connecticut.

**Rachelle Loyear** has spent over a decade managing various projects and programs in corporate security organizations, focusing strongly on business continuity and organizational resilience. In her work life, she has directed teams responsible for ensuring resilience in the face of many different types of security risks, both physical and logical. Her responsibilities have included: Security/BCM program design and development; crisis management and emergency response planning; functional and location-based recovery and continuity planning; crisis management and continuity training and operational continuity exercises; and logistical programs, such as public/private partnership relationship management and crisis recovery resource programs.

She began her career in information technology (IT), working in programming and training design at an online training company, prior before moving into the telecommunications industry. She has worked in various IT roles – including Web design, user experience, business analysis, and project management – before moving into the security/business continuity arena. This diverse background enables her to approach security, risk, business continuity, and disaster recovery with a broad methodology that melds many aspects into a cohesive whole.

Rachelle holds a bachelor's degree in history from the University of North Carolina at Charlotte, and a master's degree in business administration from the University of Phoenix. She is certified as a Master Business Continuity Professional (MBCP) through DRI International, as an Associate Fellow of Business Continuity International (AFBCI), as a Certified Information Security Manager (CISM) through ISACA, and as a Project Management Professional (PMP) through the Project Management Institute (PMI). She is active in multiple BCM industry groups and is vice-chair of the Crisis Management and Business Continuity Council of ASIS International as well as serving on the IT Security Council.

# New eBooks
## *From The Rothstein Publishing eBook Collection*

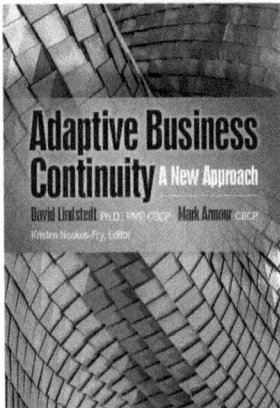

### Adaptive Business Continuity: A New Approach
**David Lindstedt, Ph.D., PMP, CBCP and and Mark Armour, CBCP**
Kristen Noakes-Fry, ABCI, Editor
*(A Rothstein Publishing Collection eBook)* June 2017
ISBN: 978-1-944480-4-0 (EPUB)
ISBN: 978-1-944480-41-7 (PDF)
172 pages

The preparedness planning industry is at a turning point. Circumstances demand that professionals look at business continuity (BC) and its practice in new ways. Adaptive Business Continuity: A New Approach offers an alternative to make your BC program more effective. Adaptive Business Continuity will improve your organization's recovery capabilities.

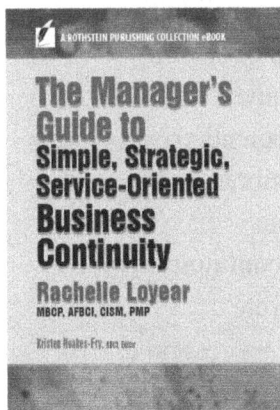

### The Manager's Guide to Simple, Stategic, Service-Oriented Business Continuity
**Rachelle Loyear, MBCP, AFBCI, CISM, PMP**  Kristen Noakes-Fry, ABCI, Editor
*(A Rothstein Publishing Collection eBook)* May 2017
ISBN: 978-1-944480-38-7 (EPUB)
ISBN: 978-1-944480-39-4 (PDF)
145 pages

You have the knowledge and skill to create a workable Business Continuity Management (BCM) program –but too often, your projects are stalled while you attempt to get the right information from the right person. Rachelle Loyear takes you through the practical steps to get your program back on track.

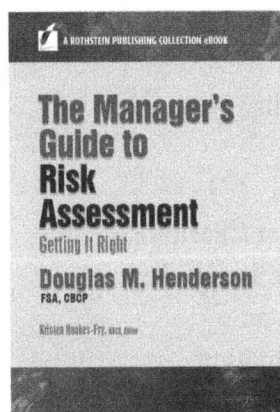

### The Manager's Guide to Risk Assessment: Getting It Right
**Douglas M. Henderson,  FSA, CBCP** Kristen Noakes-Fry, ABCI, Editor
(A Rothstein Publishing Collection eBook) March 2017
ISBN: 978-1-944480-38-7 (EPUB)
ISBN: 978-1-944480-39-4 (PDF)
114 pages

Risk assessment is required for just about all business plans or decisions. As a responsible manager, you need to consider threats to your organization's resilience. But to determine probability and impact – and reduce your risk – can be a daunting task. Guided by Henderson's The Manager's Guide to Risk Assessment: Getting It Right, you will confidently follow a clearly explained, step-by-step process to conduct a risk assessment.

**ROTHSTEIN PUBLISHING**
A Division of Rothstein Associates Inc.

Brookfield, Connecticut USA
www.rothstein.com

f www.facebook.com/RothsteinPublishing

in www.linkedin.com/company/rothsteinpublishing

y www.twitter.com/rothsteinpub

I

# New eBooks

## *From The Rothstein Publishing eBook Collection*

### The Manager's Guide to Cybersecurity Law: Essentials for Today's Business

**Teri Schreider, SSCP, SISM, C | CISO, ITIL Foundation**  Kristen Noakes-Fry, ABCI, Editor
(A Rothstein Publishing Collection eBook) February 2017
ISBN: 978-1-944480-30-1 (EPUB)
ISBN: 978-1-944480-31-8 (PDF)
168 pages

In today's litigious business world, cyber-related matters could land you in court. As a computer security professional, you are protecting your data, but are you protecting your company? While you know industry standards and regulations, you may not be a legal expert, but fortunately, in a few hours of reading rather than months of classroom study you could be.

### The Manager's Guide to Enterprise Security Risk Management: Essentials of Risk-Based Security

**Brian J. Allen, Esq., CISSP, CISM, CPP, CFE**
**Rachelle Loyear MBCP, AFBCI, CISM, PMP**  Kristen Noakes-Fry, ABCI, Editor
(A Rothstein Publishing Collection eBook) November 2016
ISBN: 978-1-944480-24-0 (EPUB)
ISBN: 978-1-944480-25-7 (PDF)

Is security management changing so fast that you can't keep up? Perhaps it seems like those traditional "best practices" in security no longer work? One answer might be that you need better best practices!

### The Manager's Guide to Business Continuity Exercises: Testing Your Plan

**Jim Burtles, KLT, MMLT, Hon FBCI**  Kristen Noakes-Fry, ABCI, Editor
(A Rothstein Publishing Collection eBook) November 2016
ISBN: 978-1-944480-32-5 (EPUB)
ISBN: 978-1-944480-33-2 (PDF)
100 pages

Your challenge is to maintain a good and effective plan in the face of changing circumstances and limited budgets. If your situation is like that in most companies, you really cannot depend on the results of last year's test or exercise of the plan.

## ROTHSTEIN PUBLISHING
A Division of Rothstein Associates Inc.

Brookfield, Connecticut USA
www.rothstein.com

www.facebook.com/RothsteinPublishing

www.linkedin.com/company/rothsteinpublishing

www.twitter.com/rothsteinpub

II

# New eBooks
## *From The Rothstein Publishing eBook Collection*

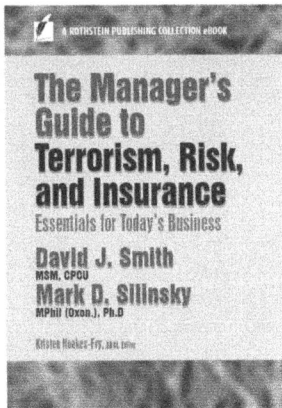

### The Manager's Guide to Terrorism, Risk, & Insurance: Essentials for Today's Business
**David J. Smith, MSM, CPCU  Mark D. Silinsky, MPhol (Oxon.), Ph.D**
Kristen Noakes-Fry, ABCI, Editor
(A Rothstein Publishing Collection eBook) October 2016
ISBN: 978-1-944480-26-4 (EPUB)
ISBN: 978-1-944480-27-1 (PDF)
120 pages

As a manager, you're aware of terrorist acts, are considering the risks, but sense that you need more background. How might terrorism occur?

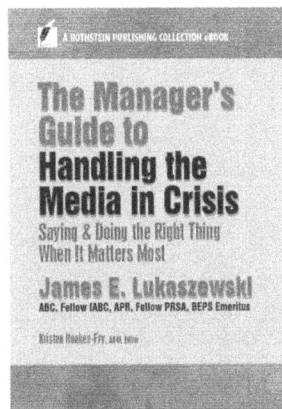

### The Manager's Guide to Handling the Media in a Crisis: Saying & Doing the Right Thing When It Matters Most
**James E. Lukaszewski, ABC, Fellow IABC, Fellow PRSA, BEPS Emeritus**
Kristen Noakes-Fry, ABCI, Editor
(A Rothstein Publishing Collection eBook) September 2016
ISBN: 978-1-944480-28-8 (EPUB)
ISBN: 978-1-944480-29-5 (PDF)
120 pages

Attracting media attention is surprisingly easy – you just want it to be the right kind! If an event causes the phone to ring and TV cameras to appear in your lobby, you need confidence that the people who happen to be at your worksite that day are prepared.

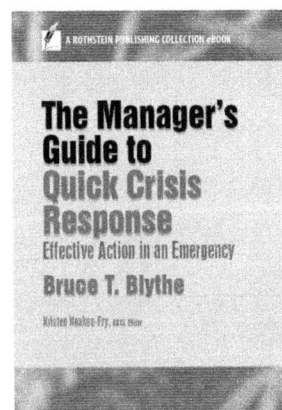

### The Manager's Guide to Quick Crisis Response: Effective Action in an Emergency
**Bruce T. Blythe**  Kristen Noakes-Fry, ABCI, Editor
(A Rothstein Publishing Collection eBook) August 2016
ISBN: 978-1-944480-23-3 (EPUB)
ISBN: 978-1-944480-22-6 (PDF)
117 pages

Avoid being "blindsided" by an unexpected emergency or crisis in the workplace – violence, natural disaster, or worse!

**ROTHSTEIN PUBLISHING**
A Division of Rothstein Associates Inc.
Brookfield, Connecticut USA
www.rothstein.com

f www.facebook.com/RothsteinPublishing
in www.linkedin.com/company/rothsteinpublishing
y www.twitter.com/rothsteinpub

# New eBooks
## *From The Rothstein Publishing eBook Collection*

### The Manager's Guide to Cybersecurity Law: Essentials for Today's Business
**Teri Schreider, SSCP, SISM, C | CISO, ITIL Foundation** Kristen Noakes-Fry, ABCI, Editor
(A Rothstein Publishing Collection eBook) February 2017
ISBN: 978-1-944480-30-1 (EPUB)
ISBN: 978-1-944480-31-8 (PDF)
168 pages

In today's litigious business world, cyber-related matters could land you in court. As a computer security professional, you are protecting your data, but are you protecting your company? While you know industry standards and regulations, you may not be a legal expert, but fortunately, in a few hours of reading rather than months of classroom study you could be.

### The Manager's Guide to Enterprise Security Risk Management: Essentials of Risk-Based Security
**Brian J. Allen, Esq., CISSP, CISM, CPP, CFE**
**Rachelle Loyear MBCP, AFBCI, CISM, PMP** Kristen Noakes-Fry, ABCI, Editor
(A Rothstein Publishing Collection eBook) November 2016
ISBN: 978-1-944480-24-0 (EPUB)
ISBN: 978-1-944480-25-7 (PDF)

Is security management changing so fast that you can't keep up? Perhaps it seems like those traditional "best practices" in security no longer work? One answer might be that you need better best practices!

### The Manager's Guide to Business Continuity Exercises: Testing Your Plan
**Jim Burtles, KLT, MMLT, Hon FBCI** Kristen Noakes-Fry, ABCI, Editor
(A Rothstein Publishing Collection eBook) November 2016
ISBN: 978-1-944480-32-5 (EPUB)
ISBN: 978-1-944480-33-2 (PDF)
100 pages

Your challenge is to maintain a good and effective plan in the face of changing circumstances and limited budgets. If your situation is like that in most companies, you really cannot depend on the results of last year's test or exercise of the plan.

## ROTHSTEIN PUBLISHING
A Division of Rothstein Associates Inc.
Brookfield, Connecticut USA
www.rothstein.com

f www.facebook.com/RothsteinPublishing

in www.linkedin.com/company/rothsteinpublishing

www.twitter.com/rothsteinpub

# New eBooks
## *From The Rothstein Publishing eBook Collection*

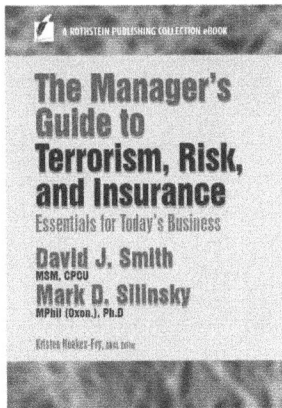

### The Manager's Guide to Terrorism, Risk, & Insurance: Essentials for Today's Business
**David J. Smith, MSM, CPCU  Mark D. Silinsky, MPhol (Oxon.), Ph.D**
Kristen Noakes-Fry, ABCI, Editor
(A Rothstein Publishing Collection eBook) October 2016
ISBN: 978-1-944480-26-4 (EPUB)
ISBN: 978-1-944480-27-1 (PDF)
120 pages

As a manager, you're aware of terrorist acts, are considering the risks, but sense that you need more background. How might terrorism occur?

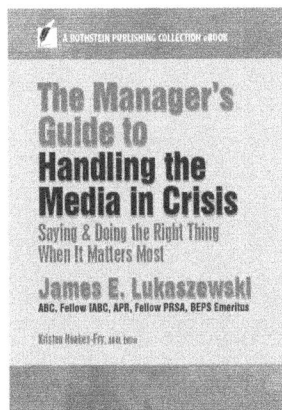

### The Manager's Guide to Handling the Media in a Crisis: Saying & Doing the Right Thing When It Matters Most
**James E. Lukaszewski, ABC, Fellow IABC, Fellow PRSA, BEPS Emeritus**
Kristen Noakes-Fry, ABCI, Editor
(A Rothstein Publishing Collection eBook) September 2016
ISBN: 978-1-944480-28-8 (EPUB)
ISBN: 978-1-944480-29-5 (PDF)
120 pages

Attracting media attention is surprisingly easy – you just want it to be the right kind! If an event causes the phone to ring and TV cameras to appear in your lobby, you need confidence that the people who happen to be at your worksite that day are prepared.

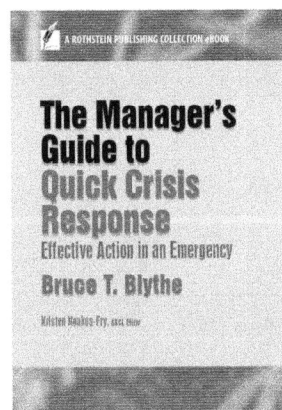

### The Manager's Guide to Quick Crisis Response: Effective Action in an Emergency
**Bruce T. Blythe**  Kristen Noakes-Fry, ABCI, Editor
(A Rothstein Publishing Collection eBook) August 2016
ISBN: 978-1-944480-23-3 (EPUB)
ISBN: 978-1-944480-22-6 (PDF)
117 pages

Avoid being "blindsided" by an unexpected emergency or crisis in the workplace – violence, natural disaster, or worse!

ROTHSTEIN PUBLISHING
A Division of Rothstein Associates Inc.

Brookfield, Connecticut USA
www.rothstein.com

f www.facebook.com/RothsteinPublishing

in www.linkedin.com/company/rothsteinpublishing

y www.twitter.com/rothsteinpub

# New eBooks
## *From The Rothstein Publishing eBook Collection*

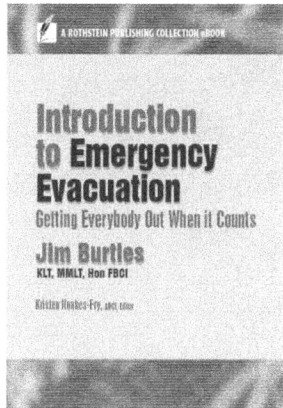

### Introduction to Emergency Evacuation: Getting Everybody Out When It Counts

**Bruce T. Blythe** Kristen Noakes-Fry, ABCI, Editor
(A Rothstein Publishing Collection eBook) July 2016 ISBN: 978-1-944480-14-1 (EPUB)
ISBN: 978-1-944480-15-8 (PDF)
120 pages

When it's not just a drill, you need to get it right the first time. If an emergency alert sounds, are you ready to take charge and get everyone out of the office, theater, classroom, or store safely?

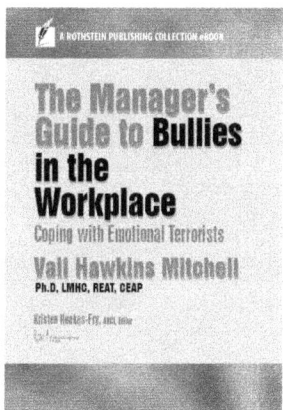

### The Manager's Guide to Bullies in the Workplace: Coping with Emotional Terrorists

**Vali Hawkins Mitchell, Ph.D, LMHC, REAT, CEAP** Kristen Noakes-Fry, ABCI, Editor
(A Rothstein Publishing Collection eBook) July 2016
ISBN: 978-1-944480-12-7 (EPUB)
ISBN: 978-1-944480-13-4 (PDF)
120 pages

As a manager, you can usually handle disruptive employees. But sometimes, their emotional states foster workplace tension, even making them a danger to others.

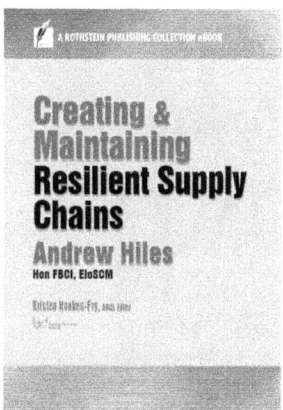

### Creating & Maintaining Resilient Supply Chains

**Andrew Hiles, Hon FBCI, EloSCM** Kristen Noakes-Fry, ABCI, Editor
(A Rothstein Publishing Collection eBook) July 2016
ISBN: 978-1-944480-07-3 (EPUB)
ISBN: 978-1-944480-08-0 (PDF)
120 pages

Will your supply chain survive the twists and turns of the global economy? Can it deliver mission-critical supplies and services in the face of disaster or other business interruption?

**ROTHSTEIN PUBLISHING**
A Division of Rothstein Associates Inc.
Brookfield, Connecticut USA
www.rothstein.com

f www.facebook.com/RothsteinPublishing

in www.linkedin.com/company/rothsteinpublishing

y www.twitter.com/rothsteinpub

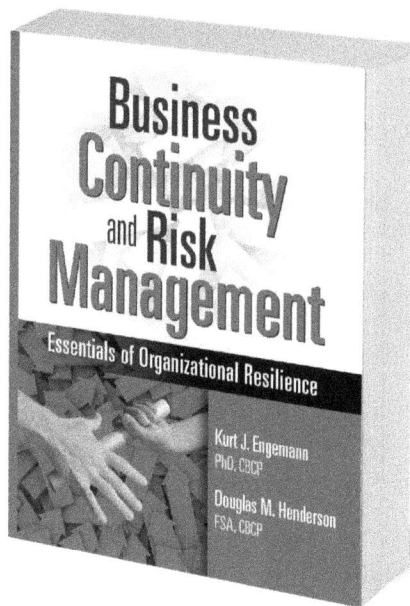

### State-of-the-Art Exposition of the "Twin Disciplines"
### Business Continuity and Risk Management:
Essentials of Organizational Resilience
By Kurt J. Engemann, PhD, CBCP and Douglas M. Henderson, FSA, CBCP

Business Continuity and Risk Management are now considered twin disciplines and this new text offers a state-of-the-art exposition of the global body of knowledge for their interrelationship.

> » 10 chapters cover Business Continuity principles and practices; 3 focus on Information Technology and Emergency Management; and 4 explain Risk Modeling for those wanting statistical underpinnings in Risk Management.

> » Extensive Instructor Resources are available for college courses and professional development training, including syllabi, test bank, discussion questions, case studies, and slides.

Authors are a college professor who is also editor-in-chief of the International Journal of Business Continuity and Risk Management, and a Business Continuity consultant with 25+ years of experience.

*"It's difficult to write a book that serves both academia and practitioners, but this text provides a firm foundation for novices and a valuable reference for experienced professionals."*
— Security Management Magazine

©2012, 370 pages, glossary, index  ISBN 978-1-931332-54-5, paperback 8.5 x 11
ISBN 978-1-931332-73-6, PDF/eBook   ISBN 978-1-931332-89-7, ePub

---

### Demonstrates That Systematically Managing Individual and Collective Workplace Emotions Is Critical to Risk and Crisis Management
### The Cost of Emotions in the Workplace:
The Bottom Line Value of Emotional Continuity Management
By Vali Hawkins Mitchell, PhD, LMHC

Finally — a people management guide that goes way beyond the typical "problem employee" books to help you understand and manage the entire emotional culture of your organization.

> » Introduces the rising field of Emotional Continuity Management (ECM) and provides a tested system to observe, predict, prepare, and write policy to manage the full range of workplace emotions productively — to stop workplace problems before they start.

> » Offers tools to quantify bottom-line costs of disruptive emotional incidents, from bad managers, emotional terrorists and office bullies to workplace violence, and includes real-life examples, tips, tools, checklists, forms, and sample plans.

**"Dr. Vali"** is a Certified Traumatologist, holds a Doctorate in Health Education, and is a highly regarded speaker, consultant, educator, and counselor to victims of major disasters, including 9/11 and Hurricane Katrina.

*"You'll look with new eyes at the enormous role played by human emotions in today's business. I endorse it as a guide for the 21st century global workforce."*
— James J. Cappola, MD, PhD, Medical Director, Medical Affairs, Harvard Clinical Research Institute

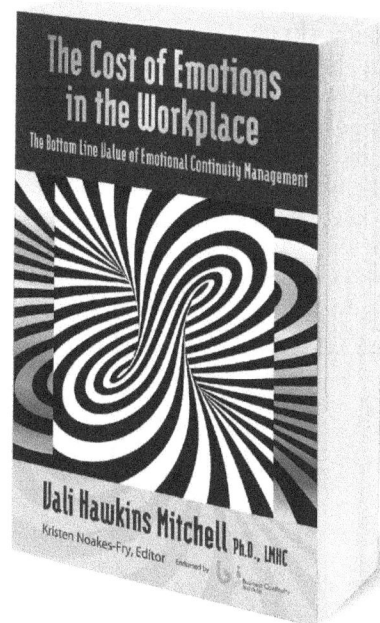

©2013, 300 pages, glossary, index ISBN 978-1-931332-58-3, paperback 6x9   ISBN 978-1-931332-68-2 PDF/eBook
ISBN 978-1-931332-84-2 ePub

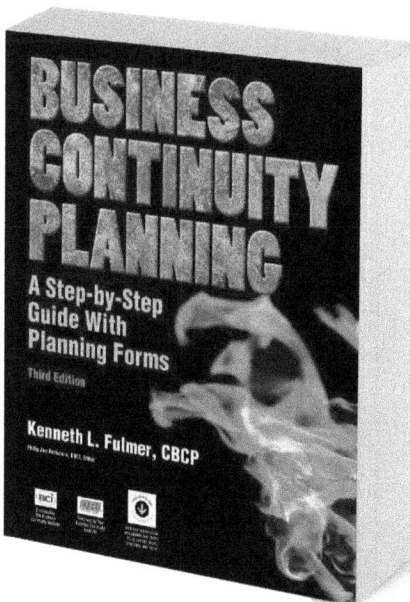

---

### Easy Workbook Format Shows Managers New to Business Continuity Planning How to Develop a Basic Plan and Keep It Updated
### Business Continuity Planning:
A Step-by-Step Guide with Planning Forms, 3rd Edition
By Ken Fulmer, CBCP

If you've been tasked with developing a basic business continuity plan and aren't sure where to start, this workbook with sample forms, checklists, and plans will walk you step-by-step through the process.

> » Extensive, easy to-use downloadable resources include reproducible worksheets, forms, templates, questionnaires, and checklists for various natural disasters and special hazards such as power outages, boiler failures, bomb threats, hazardous material spills, and civil unrest, along with a checklist for vital records storage.

> » Straightforward explanations emphasize non-technical aspects of Business Continuity Planning/Disaster Recovery.

**Kenneth L. Fulmer**, a 30+ year veteran of the computer industry, has published, trained and spoken on business continuity throughout his career.

*"This excellent primer sets out a simple, concise, and, most of all, logical roadmap both for developing the justification for a business continuity/disaster recovery program as well as for developing and maintaining the resultant plan."*
— Larry Kalmis, FBCI, Project Executive, Virtual Corporation and Chairman, Business Continuity Institute

©2008, 190 pages, + Downloadable Resources, glossary  ISBN 978-1931332-21-7, paperback 8.5 x 11
ISBN: 978-1-931332-80-4, PDF/eBook  ISBN: 978-1-931332-90-3, ePub

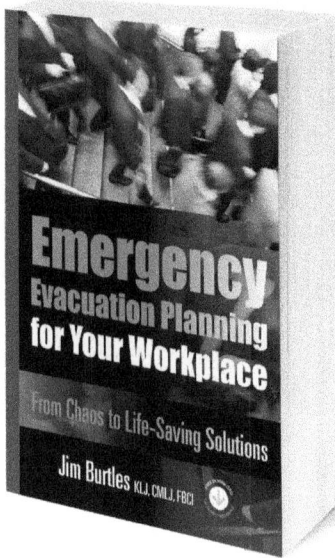

## First All-in-One, Practical Resource That Integrates Workplace Emergency Evacuation Planning with Business Continuity

### Emergency Evacuation Planning for Your Workplace:
From Chaos to Life-Saving Solutions
By Jim Burtles, KLJ, CMLJ, FBCI

Whether you work in facilities management, HR, or emergency, risk and business continuity management, this groundbreaking new book will become your go-to resource for safely evacuating people of all ages and health conditions from workplaces of all kinds.

» Based on 12 years' research into global best practices, it includes a comprehensive package of 600+ pages of book and downloadable resources with tools, templates, case studies, sample plans, forms, checklists, articles, and practical tips.

» Selected by the International Facilities Management Association (IFMA) and endorsed by The Business Continuity Institute (BCI).

**Jim Burtles** is an internationally acclaimed Business Continuity consultant with 35 years' experience in 24 countries. A founding Fellow of the Business Continuity Institute, he received BCI's Lifetime Achievement Award in 2001.

*"Unique, comprehensive, important guide and reference for anyone interested in workplace safety and emergency evacuation planning. Recommended."*
— Choice Magazine, Association of College and Research Libraries

©2013, 340 pages + Downloadable Resources, glossary, index  ISBN 978-1-931332-56-9, casebound 6x9
ISBN 978-1-931332-67-5, PDF/eBook  ISBN: 978-1-931332-85-9, ePub

## Selected One of "30 Best Business Books of 2013" by Soundview Executive Book Summaries

### Lukaszewski on Crisis Communication: What Your CEO Needs to Know About Reputation Risk and Crisis Management
By James E. Lukaszewski, ABC, APR, Fellow PRSA

*America's Crisis Guru* draws on four decades of consulting experience confronting crises of every kind to advise you exactly what to do, what to say, when to say it, and when to do it while the whole world is watching. He uniquely emphasizes how to manage the victim-driven nature of crisis.

» Tells how to get heard by management and gives step-by-step details for creating a practical crisis communication plan and putting it into action in the real world of victims, media relations, social media, litigation, and activists.

» Packed with case studies/examples, practical tools, charts, checklists, forms, and templates.

**James E. Lukaszewski** (loo-ka-SHEV-skee), profiled in Living Legends of American Public Relations, was invited by Penn State University to speak at its 2013 Bronstein Lecture in Ethics and Public Relations and was recognized by the Minnesota Chapter of Public Relations Society of America with the Donald G. Padilla Distinguished Practitioner Award for his role as a PR educator, ethicist, and ambassador.

*"Jim is one of the most knowledgeable people on earth about crisis management and his counsel has saved the reputation of many corporations and individuals."*
— Jay Rayburn, PhD, Fellow PRSA, Division Director, Advertising/Public Relations, School of Communication, Florida State University

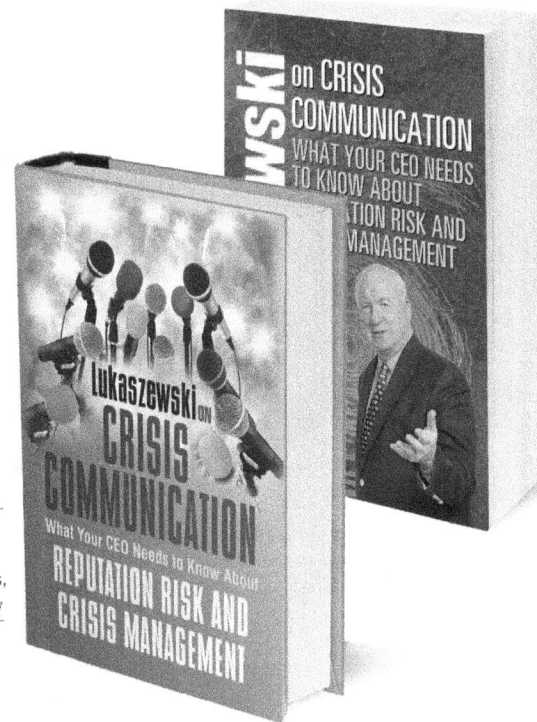

©2013, 400 pages, glossary, index  ISBN 978-1-931332-66-8, hardcover 6x9
ISBN 978-1-931332-57-6, paperback 6x9  ISBN 978-1-931332-64-4, PDF/eBook
ISBN 978-1-931332-81-1, ePub

## Selected by Risk and Insurance Management Society (RIMS) and American Society for Quality (ASQ)

### Root Cause Analysis Handbook:
A Guide to Efficient and Effective Incident Investigation, 3rd Edition
By ABS Consulting; Lee N. Vanden Heuvel, Donald K. Lorenzo, Laura O. Jackson, Walter E. Hanson, James J. Rooney, and David A. Walker

Reach for this bestselling handbook anytime you need to identify and eliminate the root cause of incidents with quality, reliability, production processes, and environmental, health, and safety impacts – and their attendant risks.

» THE most complete, all-in-one package available for root cause analysis, including 600+ pages of book and downloadable resources; color-coded, 17" x 22" Root Cause Map™; and licensed access to extensive online resources.

» Based on a globally successful, proprietary methodology developed by an international consulting firm with 50 years' experience in 35 countries.

*A global classic called "in a league of its own" and "the best resource on the subject."*

©2008, 300 pages + Downloadable Resources, fold-out map, glossary  ISBN 978-1-931332-51-4, paperback 8.5x11
ISBN 978-1-931332-72-9, PDF/eBook,  ISBN 978-1-931332-82-8, PDF/eBook